MENTOR YOUR MIND

TESTED MANTRAS FOR THE BUSY WOMAN

ALSO BY MAMTA SINGH

- MIGRAINES FOR THE INFORMED WOMAN
  Tips from a sufferer
- THE URBAN WOMAN'S INTEGRATED FITNESS GUIDE

Disclaimer

Readers are advised to consult their doctor/clinical psychologist/psychiatrist or any other qualified health professional before embarking on any of the activities, exercises, routines, advice etc. given in the book. All advise are subject to the reader acquiring a clearance from the doctor/clinical psychologist/psychiatrist or health provider that they are healthy, do not suffer from physical conditions and that the doctor has no objection to the reader starting the activities suggested in the book.

Despite the advances of modern science and medicine, the human mind still remains an enigma to mankind. The realms of the working and behaviour of our mind and treatments to restore equilibrium during times of imbalance is an evolving science and views held by doctors and researchers change with the passage of time. This book is NOT a medical advice.

MENTOR YOUR MIND

TESTED MANTRAS FOR THE BUSY WOMAN

MAMTA SINGH

Holistic Health Therapist – SAC Dip (UK)
Aerobics Instructor, Personal Trainer – IFA (USA)
Sports Nutritionist – IFA (USA)

Sterling Paperbacks

STERLING PAPERBACKS
An imprint of
Sterling Publishers (P) Ltd.
A-59, Okhla Industrial Area, Phase-II, New Delhi-110020.
Tel: 26387070, 26386209; Fax: 91-11-26383788
E-mail: mail@sterlingpublishers.com
www.sterlingpublishers.com

Mentor Your Mind
© 2011, Mamta Singh
ISBN 978 81 207 5973 2

All rights are reserved.
No part of this publication may be reproduced, stored in a retrieval system or transmitted, in any form or by any means, mechanical, photocopying, recording or otherwise, without prior written permission of the author.

Printed in India

Printed and Published by Sterling Publishers Pvt. Ltd., New Delhi-110 020.

TO CKO

Who walked every step of the long, winding and ill-lit road with me,
I dedicate this book to you.

Contents

MENTAL FITNESS

1. The Disturbing Truth, Overt Offenders – The 10 minute questionnaire — 3
   - What I mean by mental fitness
   - Results of reality check and the shocking truth!
   - Your stealthy and stark suspects
   - How mental fitness integrates into your life
   - How mentally fit are you?

2. Positive Psychology: Weapon against the sinister six — 16
   - Afflicted with anxiety
   - The lashings of lay-offs
   - The nuisance of negation
   - The pressure of parental care
   - The stressful saga of socializing
   - The woes of weight

3. Meditation: Tune in and out at will — 48
   - Meditation for relaxation
   - Meditation for improving focus

4. Physical Exercises to Stub Stress — 53
   - On the run – intermediate level treadmill workout with built-in intervals
   - Take a ride – intermediate level stationary bike workout with built-in intervals
   - Other roads to mental fitness

Contents

5. How Can You Tell it's Time to See a Doctor   60
   - Answering your questions
   - Indicators that point to seeking professional help
   - 10 Things you need to know before you fix that appointment
   - Options in medication
   - In conclusion
   - Daily dozen - activities that keep your brain ticking

EMOTIONAL FITNESS

6. Through the Barricades to Meet Yourself   77
   - Evolution of emotional fitness into emotional wellness
   - Emotional, physical and mental fitness – the awesome threesome!
   - The 15-minute self-evaluation of emotions
7. Erasing the Emotional Scars – Tackling the sticky six   84
   - Abridging anger
   - Boredom and loneliness
   - Darkness after a death in the family
   - Dungeons of depression
   - The demons of divorce
   - Work-life balance
8. The Way Forward   125
   - Acceptance of the situation
   - Identification of your shortcomings and working a plan
   - Re-tuning
   - Unconditional love
9. Living in Emotional Wellness   135

SPIRITUAL FITNESS

10. Spirituality in Cyber Age — 143
    - Why should you be spiritually fit?
    - The search for values
    - The 5 minutes towards self-observation – a questionnaire

11. Grounding Yourself in Spiritual Fitness — 152
    - Clean a school or the neighbourhood
    - Community work and karma
    - Cook and serve food at orphanages
    - Donate knowledge at orphanages etc.
    - Give away time – old age homes and rehab centres
    - Helping the handicapped at special schools
    - Meditation and stillness

12. Inner Equanimity: A daily routine — 163

    Bibliography — 169

Preface

Mentor Your Mind was born at the time I was still writing my second book, The Urban Woman's Integrated Fitness Guide. While that book had a physical fitness focus, my mind already knew what needed to follow, so that both my own and the reader's endeavour towards achieving total health were at the tips of our finger whenever we needed them.

Unlike computer architecture, the blueprint and the operational structure of the human body has been designed following a hierarchical pattern. As our brain and mind are the controlling units for all conscious and sub-conscious processes, it is no wonder it is placed at the top of the body. Evolution has taken care of this aspect in most of the animals we see. With plants, the order is almost reversed.

Today, we are well aware that though keeping a healthy body is an option, yet it is not enough. Each one of us knows of people in our lives who have been 'physically fit', done their workouts, eaten the right foods and yet succumbed to diseases like cardiac arrests and cancers etc. So while the muscles were powerful and toned, the mind was engulfed in stress and beset in conditions that proved the silent killer and lent the fatal blow.

More than at any other times of our lives, our minds need detoxification treatments as much, if not more, than our bodies. Living through the days, weeks, years and sometimes even decades of suppressed anger, stress and frustration at life's handouts, muting our inner voice and eventually turning numb to feelings makes us lose contact with our own self. Over a period of time, we function at a very basic level not able to extract what the 'whole' is capable of giving and supporting in us.

There are many simple and not so simple perspectives to mind study, such as those of Philosophies of mind, Science of mind, mental health and the new age alternative perspectives etc. And while there is no dearth in the availability of literature on mind concepts and healthy living, there seems to be paucity in the linkages offered between what a particular practice or tip will do for you at a mental, emotional or physical level.

In this book, I have kept my focus on the cause–effect relation in the realms of mental health through a mix of what is easily fathomable and achievable by you. These will include everyday practice tips, activities, simple yoga, easy meditation and service, all of which are do-able for a modern day woman and those that easily fit into her busy day and that which does not demand setting precious time aside for being mentally, emotionally and spiritually healthy.

Within the pages of **Mentor Your Mind**, I have put together literature, some of which I have personally practiced on myself as a student of life and living, and gained immensely and almost immediately from. If you are looking for the missing pieces in your life despite living a seemingly 'good' life or even an unbalanced or a stymied one, this may be the book for you.

22nd February, 2011   Yours in Health and Fitness
Qatar   **Mamta Singh**
fullbloomfreelance@gmail.com

MENTAL FITNESS

"The Mind loves the nonessential; it is always hungry for gossip and self-deprecation. Something utterly useless and it listens so attentively."

Osho (1931-1990)
Spiritual Guru

The Disturbing Truth, Overt Offenders – The 10 minute questionnaire

So much has been spoken about and written on the subject of physical fitness that it feels almost sacred to be presenting a book on mental fitness. Much as you would see television channels and bookstore shelves replete with material on how to keep the body looking divine, you may find it hard to come across a channel on radio or television that tells you how to stop those voices in your head even while you are running on your treadmill.

Bookshelf space in stores gives a perfunctory 15% of their total health space to books that deal with mental peace. This 15% space will inevitably be taken by a mix of Yoga and meditation books along with heavy reading from Ph.D. gurus on the matter of mental disorders and interaction skills. Though I do agree that these are a part of total mental health, most are either difficult for the user to comprehend or not easy to implement in their busy living. And then again, they only reflect a fragment of the whole story.

To keep the heavy jargon at bay and give you some interesting thoughts you can play with, I have in the following pages, provided self-scoring, easy to understand questionnaires, few but effective techniques to try and test in your everyday living, so that you feel the difference in your quality of thoughts in a short period of time and feel the need to experiment more. In places where terminology cannot be avoided, I have tried to keep the esoteric out by explaining the rationale behind it and with examples, so that you may find this book easy to use and grow with.

What I mean by mental fitness

Before I begin with the term mental fitness, which can be most easily understood as a state of mental wellbeing, it is important to appreciate what mental health is. Mental fitness is a derivative of mental health.

For the layperson, any individual who can use their cognitive and emotional capabilities to meet the day-to-day demands of everyday life can be considered mentally healthy. This implies the person to be in a state of psychological and emotional well-being to achieve the end of meeting the ordinary demands of life successfully.

A technical but comprehensive definition of mental health readily comes from Diane and Robert Hales, as "*the capacity to think rationally and logically and to cope with the transitions, stresses, traumas, and losses that occur in all lives, in ways that allow emotional stability and growth. In general, mentally healthy individuals value themselves, perceive reality as it is, accept its limitations and possibilities, respond to its challenges, carry out their responsibilities, establish and maintain close relationships, deal reasonably with others, pursue work that suits their talent and training, and feel a sense of fulfilment that makes the efforts of daily living worthwhile.*"[1]

You can see from the definition above that there is an element of including your ability to adapt to the environmental stresses and your capability to work productively at home or away with others or alone. People in good mental health are also the ones who try and improve the state of the society they live and interact in apart from their own personal condition.

---

1. World Health Organization (1998). *World Health Report 1998: Life in the Twenty-first Century, A Vision for All.* (p 34), Report of the Director-General. Geneva: Author.

It is thus easy to see that mental fitness includes more than just an absence of mental or psychological disorder.

If you say yes to a majority of the questions listed here, you can comfortably consider yourself to be mentally healthy.

> 1. In any community set up (a social gathering, a charity event or at office), do you find it easy to cooperate with others and work as a part of the team?
> 2. Are you in a sustained, close relationship for more than 2 years with the same person?
> 3. Do you have at least one close friend you can depend upon, other than your partner or spouse?
> 4. Are you able to amicably and satisfactorily deal with everyday life's challenges?
> 5. Do you critically appraise yourself once every 4-6 months and see what action needs to be taken for a way forward?
> 6. Are you accepting of other's view points, perspectives, cultures and norms to include them in your lives, regardless of what you think of them personally?

If the answers to at least four of these questions are in the positive, you are in the safe zone. If not, you are most likely vulnerable to potential mental 'un-health'. I use the term 'un-health' as most things with fitness are on a relative scale. There is no perfect and absolutely mentally unhealthy. What you call fit today may improve or deteriorate marginally or substantially tomorrow. In the acceptable range come all our 'normal' and not so normal states of the mind and emotion.

Results of reality check and the shocking truth!

Prejudices against mental health, the social stigma, lack of proper awareness of treatment options as well as support groups make seven in ten Americans with conditions of mental health not receive treatment. The statistics are even more devastating for the developing world. They not only hinder proper functioning of the person affected, but also affect their economic productivity and thus the overall quality of their life.

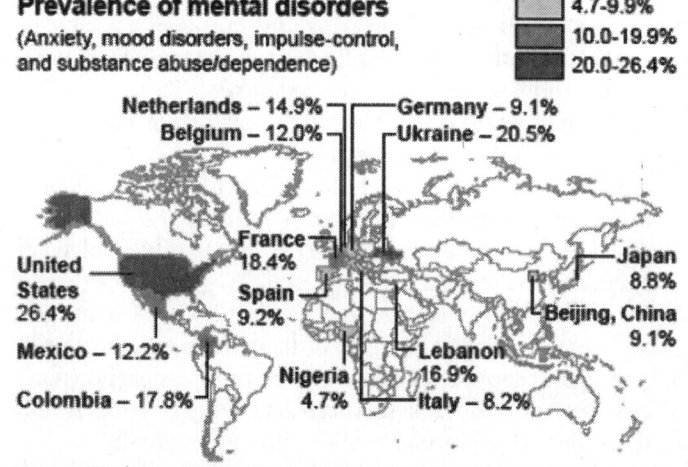

Keeping in mind the inclusion and thereby emphasis on the ability of a person towards contribution to their economy and community, to be of good mental health, the World Health Organization has defined mental health as "a state of well-being in which the individual realizes his or her own abilities, can cope with the normal stresses of life, can work productively and fruitfully, and is able to make a contribution to his or her community."[2]

There is obviously a dire need to bring about some degree of congruence between understanding as well as treatment to restore good mental health and the availability of advances to the general population at reasonable prices.

---

2. World Health Organization (2005). Promoting Mental Health: Concepts, Emerging evidence, Practice: A report of the World Health Organization, Department of Mental Health and Substance Abuse in collaboration with the Victorian Health Promotion Foundation and the University of Melbourne. World Health Organization. Geneva.

Mental afflictions such as those of mood and anxiety disorders and the more serious conditions such as PTSD (Post-Traumatic Stress Disorder) and suicidal tendencies etc. account for more than 25% of the world's total health disability issues.[3]

Issues concerning mental health are often shoved under the carpet for similar reasons of social stigma, rejection by family and loss of earning, neglect and eventually the imagined possibility of being sent into an asylum. This keeps the concerned people away from treatment facilities and psychiatric skills in the Asian continent. As Dr. Bedirhan Ustun from the WHO said, "People are reluctant to admit that they have mental problems". Because of under-reporting, there is a serious case of misallocation of treatment resources in all countries. Look at the figures for some Indian states that have been serviced by the PHC (Public Health Centres)[4] to get an idea where the government and private sector together need to plug the hole in the health services:

Mental Health Research in India

Table 1. Prevalence of Severe Mental Morbidity

	Bangalore		Baroda		Calcutta		Patiala	
Diagnosis	No. of cases	Rate/ 1000	No. of cases	Rate/ 1000	No. of cases	Rate/ 1000	No. of cases	Rate/ 1000
Epilepsy	278	7.82	51	1.28	59	1.71	11	3.17
Organic brain syndrome	4	0.11	24	0.61	22	0.64	88	2.40
Schizophrenia	65	1.83	70	1.77	71	2.05	113	3.09
Mania	20	0.56	14	0.35	8	0.23	50	1.37
Depressive Psychosis	28	0.79	22	0.55	127	3.67	150	4.10
Total no. of cases & Prevalence rate/1000	395	11.1	181	4.6	287	8.3	517	14.1
Population studied	35,548		39,665		34,582		36,595	

---

3. Taken from WHO's World Health Report, 1998.

4. Report Name: Mental Health Research in India, 2005 (Technical Monograph on ICMR Mental Health Studies), Page 10, conducted by Indian Council of Medical Research (Division of Non-communicable Diseases), Dr. Bela Shah- Senior Deputy Director General and Chief, Dr. Rashmi Parhee- Ex. Senior Research Officer Division, Dr. Narender Kumar- Deputy Director General (SG), Dr. Tripti Khanna- Asstt. Director General, Dr. Ravinder Singh- Senior Research Officer, Collated by Dr. Narender Kumar.

Your stealthy and stark suspects

If you know of any person in your life who has kept below average mental health, you will find that the reasons fall almost always in their immediate surroundings and situations. I have tried to group certain types of culprits. Though this is not a comprehensive table, it covers a good range of reasons why and how people fall prey to bad states of mental health.

Traumatic Events	Non-Trauma	Genetic	Nutrition	Substance	Origin	Others
Violence	Unemployment	Set of parental genes	Magnesium deficiency	Heavy metal poisoning	Cultural	Age
Sexual abuse	Separation from family	Twins etc.	Vitamin B12 deficiency	Substance abuse	Ethnicity	Hormonal
Military combat exposure	Death of a loved one	Inbreeding cases	Unavailable due to famine etc.		Gender	Marital status
Parental discord	Job stress		Improper food and timings			Religion
Divorce	Emotional abuse					

Whatever the reasons tabulated above, we must realize that they are very realistic ones and each one of us are potentially subject to experience one or more of them at some point of time in our lives. Some of us will be able to tackle such stress situations admirably, others will get by but quite a few of us will fall victims to the experiences which will alter their patterns of thinking, action and eventually their behaviour for life.

How mental fitness integrates into your life

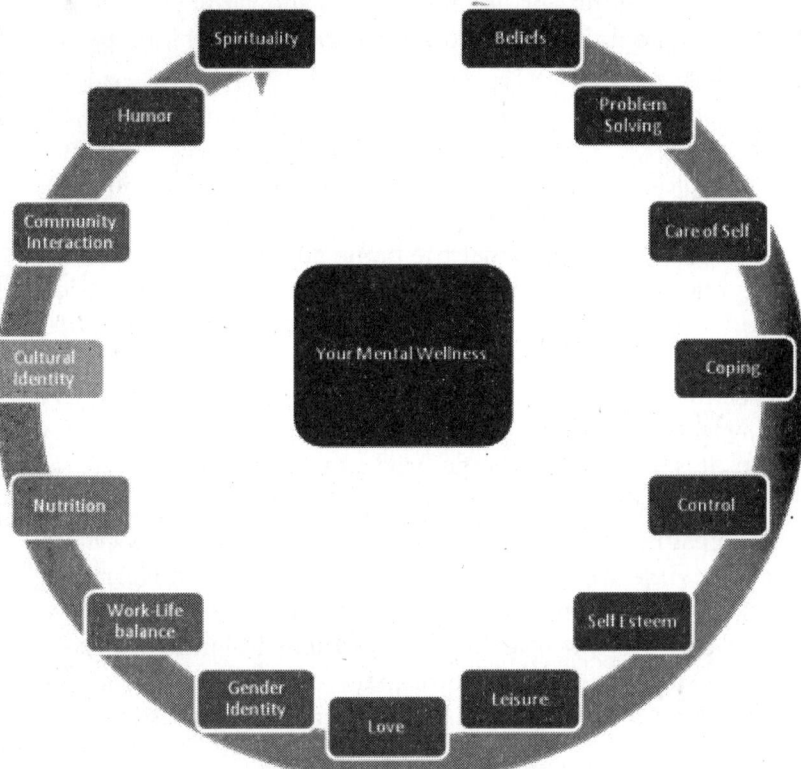

The Wheel of Mental well-being depicting its influence in every aspect of living

The Mental Wellbeing Wheel will give you a consolidated and fair notion of why you need to be mentally healthy and eventually mentally fit. Every aspect of your conscious living is intricately entwined with your mental wellbeing. In a state of good mental health, each of those elements will exhibit a positive, contended, happy or achieved status.

However, this does not imply that the vice versa is true and that if one or more elements are thrown in disarray, our mental wellbeing will be affected. Our state of mental comfort may tilt momentarily as it were, but regain equilibrium should we focus on approaches that look at your strengths, traits, emotions and weaknesses in the right perspective. You can be trained how to do this in not a very long period of time.

One popular term that has gained momentum and is of relevance at this point is 'Positive Psychology'[5]. Positive Psychology differs from positive thinking as it aims to make normal life more complete and fulfilling by nurturing talent and genius. Unlike what the name suggests, this branch is beyond plain common sense and does not reject the classical body of psychology. For these reasons it has come under critical review from the proponents of the mainstream discipline. With its modern findings in context of modern day features of wealth, human development and appreciation etc., it is increasingly being used as a valid and effective tool to heal people.

Positive psychology is of immense benefit to each one of us while we are going through both the minor irritants and major challenges of living. But before we find out how one can use those techniques to their advantage, here is my 10-minute questionnaire that I expect you to read and understand carefully and above all, answer honestly.

How mentally fit are you?

The 10-minute Questionnaire

(a) Rationale of The 10-minute Questionnaire:

I have termed the self-survey list as 'The 10-minute Questionnaire', as it contains 10 questions, which aim to size up the basic aspects of your life, your response and reaction to them. It is based on the premise that you will at the maximum

---

5. Positive Psychology is a concept proposed by Martin Seligman and Mihaly Csikszentmihalyi around 2000. They propounded it like this in their book, 'Positive Psychology, An introduction': "We believe that a psychology of positive human functioning will arise that achieves a scientific understanding and effective intervention to build thriving individuals, families, and communities."

take approximately a minute to answer each question most appropriately. To be able to do this you will need more than a couple of seconds to come close to the truth. The reading and import of the question and the provided options itself will take up approximately 10 seconds after which you can take up to a maximum of 20 seconds to check the near-reality or near-truth option. Any more time and you are either unaware or unsure what the question is trying to ask or measure.

- Questions 1 - 4 are of generic nature;
- Questions 5 - 7 relate to your personal and social facets of life;
- Questions 8 - 10 concern your professional aspects in life.

Are you ready? The next 10 minutes will reflect your level of mental health and thereby your mental fitness coefficient to a near exact degree what lengthy questionnaires used in psychological studies will gauge in an hour to only a marginal more degree of accuracy. It will also provide the basis of further exercises which I have recommended to tackle and best manage the stresses you are likely going through everyday situations. For this reason, I advise you take the questionnaire with the due significance it deserves.

I also suggest that you pick your choice of the answer for all the questions first and then go back to mark them with the score table provided on the next page. This way you will avoid the temptation to look into the scores of the following question and re-adjust your response.

(b) The 10-minute Questionnaire:

1. What is the most dominant feeling you have as you go through your day (i.e. home, personal, social and professional living)
   a. You feel you have little control and external factors control you.
   b. You feel a little satisfied that you got past at least half the chores you set out to in the morning.

c. You feel in control that you have had the day almost as you would have planned it or expected it to be.
2. You feel anxious for some reason, you are most likely to cope:
   a. With compulsive eating and drinking.
   b. With a glass of wine, movies, music and sleeping.
   c. Talking to friends and family; going for a walk or jog etc.
3. At the doctor's, you find that you are overweight by 15 pounds (approximately 6.8 kilograms) and need to reduce. You are stressed. Your most likely response would be to:
   a. Withdraw from friends, become irritable and touchy on topics of weight, vent out on friends etc.
   b. Try to regroup with friends and talk to them about your stress.
   c. Chalk out what needs to be done and do it, talk to friends for help, ideas etc. and read up material on the issue.
4. How would you describe the quality of your sleep at night?
   a. I sleep fitfully and feel tired when I awake.
   b. I sleep well most nights but don't sleep enough hours.
   c. I sleep soundly and awake refreshed.
5. One of your parents is admitted in hospital getting treated for pneumonia and you have volunteered to do hospital duty at nights. Which below best describes your temporary phase:
   a. You are wrought with worry and guilt of pending work at home and leaving family behind and it reflects on your eating and sleeping patterns.
   b. Though you are getting past the day with efficiency as can be expected at this time, you are stressed eating and not getting proper sleep.

c. You are able to get the basics done and focus that your family and parent needs you healthy more than ever now, so you eat well and exercise while at the hospital.
6. While you are home alone one late evening, you hear talking voices that seem to be coming from your kitchen garden area. Your typical response would be to:
   a. Panic and call a friend who lives close or the police.
   b. Wait a little longer to ascertain if these are just passersby in the adjoining lane.
   c. Take out your pepper spray or gun and wait.
7. At a social gathering or a party hosted by your friends, are you:
   a. The one who is sought out most to help in the kitchen?
   b. The centre of attraction and people wanted to be with you?
   c. Left alone after brief conversations with a few people?
8. Your company has announced imminent lay-offs. You would react by:
   a. Getting worked up listening to water-cooler gossip.
   b. Updating your resume and sending out to prospective employers and job agents.
   c. Gossiping, looking for job but give up exercising and eating unhealthy foods.
9. Everyone at office is overloaded with work. You have your work pre-planned and on target. Do you:
   a. Get dumped with more work from colleagues.
   b. Offer to help a select few.
   c. Demoralize others by preaching and sucking up to the boss.
10. You are passed over for promotion. You think you have put in hard work and delivered on time, shown initiative etc. and deserve better. This would have you:

a. Take up the issue with your boss professionally asking him to sight reasons for his action. If not satisfy, take up the matter with his/her boss.
b. Bitch about the situation, get demoralized, demoralize others and develop animosity with the boss not trusting any co-worker later.
c. Update and send out your resume looking for another job.

SCORE

1.	a. 0	b. 1	c. 2
2.	a. 0	b. 1	c. 2
3.	a. 0	b. 1	c. 2
4.	a. 0	b. 1	c. 2
5.	a. 0	b. 1	c. 2
6.	a. 1	b. 2	c. 0
7.	a. 1	b. 2	c. 0
8.	a. 0	b. 1	c. 2
9.	a. 0	b. 2	c. 1
10.	a. 2	b. 0	c. 1

0 – 6 You could be fire-fighting everyday living. You are overwhelmed by people and situations and feel overcome often. This category is referred to as barely (mentally) fit. You are only surviving. You could use most of the exercises and techniques suggested in this book to gain some control over your life and enjoy living.

7 -13 You are the person who is fit to enjoy life. You are good at prioritising in life and are able to enjoy personal, social and professional life on most days fairly well. On an average day, you have fair to good control on your life's priorities. In general, you are coping well and have good support in your family, friends and colleagues. However, you could look at a few suggestions to help you change so that you add variety in your techniques.

14 – 20 This is the picture of an over-achiever. You are in total control of your life. You are up to any challenges life may throw at you. You are able to achieve as a natural in the most part. However, it would be good to take the time to smell the roses as it were. Take the relaxed perspective at times. You could look at the spiritual recommendations in this book to give yourself a new leaf to explore!

The 10-minute Questionnaire will only give you a ball park indication of whether and what you can use from this book. On the assumption that most of us score anywhere between 4 and 13, I will exhibit why and how positive psychology can help us climb up a notch or two to easy living.

Positive Psychology: Weapon against the sinister six

Your scores in the 10-minute questionnaire should not be reason enough to consult a psychologist or fix an appointment with a psychiatrist who will try to undo your problem and fix your negative mental traits. You can do the 'climbing' on your own using the approach of Positive Psychology, which is a supplement of the main body of classical psychology.

You may ask why you need to befriend a new terminology and more relevantly, why and how we need to apply it or how it will benefit us. The approach of Positive Psychology will try and 'correct' any imbalance by focusing on strengths as well as weaknesses, on building the best things in life as well as repairing the worst. It will assert that both human goodness and excellence is just as authentic as distress and disorder.

This approach will utilise Seligman's parameters - positive emotions, positive individual traits, and positive institutions. It is clearly a more inclusive and holistic approach. This means that you will explore the following elements yourself through small techniques:

Positive Psychology: Weapon against the sinister six

+ Emotion	+ Individual Traits	+ Institutions
Past happiness	Strengths	Meaning of community
Present contentment	Weaknesses	Purpose of community
Future hope	Other traits	Qualities that fortify the community

Thus all such things such as virtues, capacity for love and work, courage, compassion, resilience, creativity, curiosity, integrity, self-knowledge, moderation, self-control, and wisdom, your sense of justice, responsibility, civility, parenting, nurturance, work ethic, leadership, teamwork, purpose, and tolerance will come into play. By its very nature, improvisation immediately becomes more interesting and fun! No more is the task of getting a grip on your life a tedious and often intimidating process and one that often involves therapy and medication. The trick however, is to see the signs coming in early and tackling them with the methods suggested. You've already done the first step of ascertaining where you are roughly at, through your questionnaire.

I have outlined some common situations and feelings, emotions and experiences people go through and find hard to tackle. These unbalanced responses from persons exhibit themselves in lifetimes of conditions that hamper optimal living among many of us.

1. Feeling that things are out of your control.
2. Generalised Anxiety
3. Worrying excessively about body weight issues.
4. Sleeplessness
5. The pressure of parental care.
6. Anxiety-ridden Social experiences.

7. Being disturbed with rumours of layoffs at office.
8. Finding it hard to say "No".

There are however, ways to tackle such experiences. Each one of us goes through such situations more than once in our lives. If we are able to handle such emotions in the most appropriate way, our experiences and thereby our outcomes will be worth the effort we put into cultivating the desirable practices. The trick is in adhering to the practices. Let us take a look at how some of the situations I have talked about can most desirably be handled. Of course, there is no right or best approach and practices can vary as each of us are unique in our personality, responses, etc.

1. Afflicted with anxiety

You have a big presentation tomorrow morning at office and you can't bring yourself to sleep the night before. Thoughts of possible arguments, an evaluating boss, critical colleagues and images of you presenting your work flash past your eyes. Before you know it, you get a sinking feeling, palpitations and you feel as though your mouth is parched and you feel nauseous. You try and control your worrying but it is difficult to close the floodgates of your mind. Does this sound familiar? These are the typicality of what is termed as Generalised Anxiety Disorder.

Though I have spoken of a meeting involving a presentation, the situation could be as critical as an interview that is important to you or meeting your fiancé over dinner to as non-critical as meeting your friend over a cup of coffee or an appointment with your child's teacher at school. You cross the line from healthy or 'normal' worrying about a future event to compulsively worrying about it, taking it to a new level and thereby disrupting your personal, social and professional life apart from suffering very stressful physical symptoms.

Generalised Anxiety Disorder (GAD) has a range of psycho-somatic symptoms that affect our day to day living

and restrict us to lead sub-optimal lives. It is sad that twice as many women suffer from this condition as do men. I have listed some of those symptoms that you will find easy to recognise:
1. Uncontrolled worrying about future events.
2. Uncontrolled anxiety about the happenings during the event and results thereof.
3. Frequent trouble focussing.
4. Experiencing headaches and migraines.
5. Sweaty palms and feet.
6. Being easily overwhelmed emotionally and fatigued physically.
7. Muscle stiffening.
8. Irritation and anger.
9. Tossing and turning in bed sleepless.
10. Continually feeling on the edge.
11. Prevalence of secondary conditions such as panic disorders, social and other phobia, depression, substance abuse and sometimes even OCD.

Though more often than not, your genes, hormones, brain chemicals, food you eat and your environment may be the real culprit, it still is a personal nuisance. To quote from the National Institute of Mental Health site (Government of USA), "GAD affects about 6.8 million American adults[6], including twice as many women as men.[7] The disorder develops gradually and can begin at any point in the life cycle, although the years of highest risk are between childhood and middle age. There is evidence that genes play a modest role in GAD.[8]"

---

6. Kessler RC, Chiu WT, Demler O, Walters EE. Prevalence, severity, and comorbidity of twelve-month DSM-IV disorders in the National Comorbidity Survey Replication (NCS-R). *Archives of General Psychiatry*, 2005 Jun; 62(6):617-27.

7. Robins LN, Regier DA, eds. Psychiatric disorders in America: the Epidemiologic Catchment Area Study. New York: The Free Press, 1991

8. Kendler KS, Neale MC, Kessler RC, et al. Generalized anxiety disorder in women. A population-based twin study. Archives of General Psychiatry, 1992; 49(4): 267-72.

Mentor Your Mind

Going beyond statistics, there is good news for the victims. There is a lot you can do on your own before you take the route of medication. Some cases need to evaluate themselves to see at what point they need to report to a doctor to be able to get on the path of medication. Whether or not you go the prescription drugs route, you will do good to follow some of these suggestions. They will see you through in the long run even when your medication has run its full course and you have been weaned off them.

I would go with the following schedule on a working day:

Time	To Do	Comment
5 am	Awaken and refresh	
5:15-5:30 am	1. Sit by the window or in the balcony looking out to the dawn sky. 2. Realize the vastness of the universe. 3. Focus on your breathing and heart beat.	
5:30- 6.00 am	1. Make yourself a light cup of tea or coffee. 2. Sit out with this light beverage. 3. Spend this time with yourself alone. Chalk out your night plan.	Resist the temptation to wake the kids or partner up for the daily grind.
6 – 7am	1. Performance of all morning and household chores while keeping a watch on your mind and breathing. 2. Hum to yourself in the midst of chores.	

Time	To Do	Comment
Just before leaving home for office	1. Stop. Take 2 minutes to pray. 2. Focus on the smell of flowers and incense sticks. 3. Thank God, open eyes, arise and leave slowly.	Sit on a chair in front of your God or in the prayer area. Close your eyes and pray.
While commuting to office	1. Hum a tune you like or enjoy softly. 2. Continually remind yourself that you will have a great day. 3. Tell yourself you will feel contented and safe at the end of the day in the comfort of your home and bed.	You may even choose to read a humorous book if you are riding a bus or a pool car.
At any stressful time at office	1. Assert to yourself that it is a passing phase that will last not more than a few minutes or an hour at the most. 2. Breathe deeply, quietly and in control of it.	At any time you feel unwell, you are always free to excuse yourself.
5 minutes on return	1. Sit alone anywhere in the house where you find peace. 2. Recollect on the day's events very briefly and smile at them as an observer would. 3. Breathe in and out slowly and deeply several times.	
7 – 7:30pm	1. Go for a walk alone or with someone who is free and willing.	In case this is not a possibility, you may workout at home.
8 – 8:20 pm	1. A warm bath with a few drops of Lavender oil or any essential oil you find soothing to the nerves.	
Just before bedtime--- 15 minutes	1. Keep a diary where you put in the day's very small and not so small victories, smiles and pleasures. 2. A short plan to tackle the next day's challenges head on.	

Observe how you have dedicated a minimum of 2 ½ to 3 hours on a busy working day exclusively to yourself! Had I told you to give yourself this magnitude of time every day at the start of the suggestions, you would have rolled your eyes and asked me to provide you with 'practical' suggestions. But time planned and slotted well, no more than 15 – 30 minutes is very manageable and integrated even in a busy life.

In case you are unable to keep up with all the activities, I would further recommend that you rotate the activity types given above so that you do 5 on one day and 5 different ones the next day. Without being too ambitious, even if you manage to implement 5-6 of the activities from the schedule, I would give it five stars. In case you are not able to keep an activity or two, you should not be guilty about it.

Do keep in mind you would require to adhere to this regime religiously to derive benefits even in the short time period. As with everything in life, the magic lies in persistence. There are no short cuts to personal and internal success.

2. The lashings of lay-offs

The company you have been working for over four years now is feeling the heat of the plummeting economy and decides to downsize. As rumors grip all gatherings from the coffee vending machine to the rest room, you feel dizzy with uncertainties of the future. Though much of your hopes from this company were pinned on your service time that encouraged you to make further financial commitments, the world now seems collapsing around you. It is difficult to seek comfort in colleagues as they pretty much go through the same set of emotions. Then when one morning you turn up at your desk, you find scores of your colleagues from your and other departments, divisions and branches have been served the pink slip. Suddenly you dread leaving your cubicle or returning home with the news of the inevitable happening. This is a typical first reaction to being at the receiving end of

widespread lay-offs. Here are some others which are more commonly seen in victims of downsizing:
- Numb to react on learning of your lay-off.
- Afraid and embarrassed to meet with your other colleagues
- Embarrassed to socialise outside of office
- Feeling of worthlessness
- Loss of self-esteem
- Anxiety of the uncertain future
- Experiencing withdrawal, mood swings and depression
- Suicidal and other self-afflicting injurious tendencies
- Loss of sleep
- Loss of appetite
- Sinking feeling of the heart

Though the lashings of lay-offs have affected millions across the globe adversely in the present economic downturn, it is something that can be handled, if you are prepared for it from beforehand and get organised just a little. There are a few control and a few corrective steps you could take that would make all the difference in your experience towards the nightmare of being served the pink-slip, which has even claimed several lives. Proactive behavior goes a long way!

Mentor Your Mind

At the Office:

1. It will be good (and has shown to be true on hindsight analysis given by many victims of lay-offs) if you restrain your immediate reaction to the pink-slip at the office. Immediately become aware of your emotions and how you should not be reacting here.

2. A negative or severe, unbalanced reaction will mar your chances for a job back with the firm when things return to normalcy or may even scar your references or recommendations from the HR and your boss for future employment elsewhere.
3. Do not indulge in back-biting, bitching or gossiping either. It is unlikely that any of these will help you retain the job here or find a new one elsewhere. Always be aware of unproductive and self-damaging responses. Remember, there will always be an odd colleague who would love to kick a person when his/her chips are down. Your gossip may be misquoted or ill-placed before an impressionable and influential senior by that colleague.
4. It is always better to leave the office as soon as possible. Inform your boss and HR before you leave for the day. You can return the next day more in control of your emotions and with a plan in place ready to execute.

Before Your Last Day:
1. Be polite but brief without being curt with your colleagues. They could be your colleagues in the future if you plan to continue in the same industry.
2. Clarify all your doubts with your boss without getting personal such as the reason behind your lay-off, chances of re-absorption in the future, the time period for such a re-absorption etc. Remember we require her/his technical recommendation most and possibly help with the job search if s/he is well-connected in the industry and can drop a word for you or knows where there might be suitable openings.
3. Meet with the Human Resources (HR) and Accounts staff. Collect as much information as is possible from them. You may want to know of:
   a. Severance Allowances
   b. Benefits Package

    c. Stock option redemptions if you have stake in the company
    d. References letter
    e. Help with updating the resume
    f. A letter of termination/severance/lay-off indicating reason of termination/severance/lay-off such as downsizing, cost-cutting etc.
    g. Other entitlements that require negotiating
4. Get a date and time when you can call on all these people and collect your benefits and documents.
5. Send a reminder or call to remind them of your appointment a day before visiting again so that the papers may be ready and you do not make multiple visits wasting your time.

At Home:

Thus it is easy to see that display of moderate behaviour and incorporation of planning will see you through a rough patch like those lay-offs bring with themselves. The pages that follow contain a table that exhibits how you can integrate yourself in the normal course of life even while being laid-off and use the time to develop reliable plans for yourself and your finances and include activities that you could do with family and friends for easing out the blow of a lay-off.

How To Read The Table Below:

In the table provided below, I have outlined what actions, thoughts, measures you should be taking for yourself when faced with a lay-off. This column has the header, 'You'. There will also be a cue on how your thoughts and actions should be guided towards your family. This column has the header 'Family'. What you could do at a time and situation like this with your friends is listed under the column 'Friends'. Lastly, measures you need to take towards maintaining the best financial balance given the situation you are faced with, is chalked in the column 'Finance'.

	You	Family	Friends	Finance
Integrate	• It is important you spend some time with yourself. • 'Me' time should not be a long one. • 15 minutes will do at one time. • No more than thrice a day is necessary.	• Your family will prove to be your anchor at this time, so do not break the links in embarrassment or egoistic moves. • Do things together. Read and eat together.	• This is a perfect time to network with old and current friends. • Most of them are as insecure and in need to reconnect as you are, so there is no need to feel guilty if you are reconnecting after very long. Most will welcome it.	• Getting your finance in order should be as much a priority as the other 3 elements of damage control.
Plan & Get Inputs	• Take the 'Me' time to chalk and plan. • Use a quiet corner of your house that is pleasant, well-lit and has a plant or two.	• Talk to them about your predicaments and involve them in your dilemmas. • If your children are over 10 years of age, include them in most of your conversations. This is not to put undue stress on them but to let them know the realities and their responsibilities at such a time. • Include them in decision making process so they feel worthy.	• Meeting with those in the same city is also a good idea. • This will generate more employment ideas, avenues and give you more exposure to possibilities that others may be following successfully.	• Get account statements covering the last quarter and this quarter to date from your bank. • Run the checks with your bank on credit status, premium payments on loans and health insurance, etc.

	You	Family	Friends	Finance
Heal & Act	• You can use this slot to practice controlled breathing or Pranayama. • This will help you be more in control of your emotions and hormones. • It will also keep the negativity at bay.	• Your family will give you your healing space at such a time. • You can release your emotions of sadness by crying without being judged by your partner or spouse. This is your place for healing, regrouping and receiving support.	• Meet-ups will also provide an avenue to relax and mingle – something you require in earnest at this stage. • A productive outlet of energy like this could also lead to better friendships and give you a peak into how others are handling the similar outcomes which help you fine tune your own living.	• Request a re-work of the premium payments which are most expensive such as those on the house or education or car etc. • Check if a more stretched re-payment schedule is possible which will lower the present premium load. • Do not take on more credit – they'll be difficult to pay back at this time period, biting more into your static pool of savings.

	You	Family	Friends	Finance
Create & Conserve	• Put the 'Me' time to painting, sketching, cooking, learning a new language or reading. • All creative endeavours inject your brain with positive feelings.	• You can increase both giving and receiving physical signs of affection and support like hugs and pecks. This will prove to be a healing exercise.	• Apart from providing you with comfort, these friends may also help you with finding a job and may know of vacancies or requirements around their area or in their field. • Socializing will also keep you healthily distracted from the negative and unproductive thoughts that may otherwise arise time and again about your situation.	• Make a checklist of unproductive expenses and see if you can do without them or at least reduce them. • Do leave at least room for 1 occasional extravagance so that life does not seem a challenge more than it is.
Break Routine & Work To A New Balance	• Take this 'forced' break as a break from the monotonous and mechanized living you were leading. • Follow a hobby like dancing or singing, playing the keyboard by seeking	• Maintain a normal routine with them. • In your non-focus hours, you can be out together to the park or coffee shop or any place that is not expensive and gets you out of	• This network of friends will also double up to be your support group in this time of crisis.	• See your net savings and work out how long it will last you with your current level of expenses and then at the new reduced level of expenses that

	You	Family	Friends	Finance
	inexpensive ways to pursue it.	the home for a little while.		you've worked out with your bank etc. • Re-adjust accordingly.
	• Include physical workouts. • This will keep ill-health at bay. • It will help you with feel-good hormones too. • Parks are free and available to jog or walk in and stretch without paying heftily for a gym.	• You can use the 'together time' with your partner to redraw the short and mid-term plans and work the budget together.		• Put off all high value purchases unless they start to pay in the immediate run and you see value in them worth the EMI payment.

3. The nuisance of negation

You are cooking dinner in the kitchen. It's ten minutes past seven in the evening and you are tired after office. The children are yet to return from their evening activities and the husband is in the study with his laptop. At the moment the house seems silent, yet the chatter in your head is loud with self deprecating prattle. You are thinking of the day that has just passed and as though choosing from a menu, select to pick only the ill-tasting dishes.

You wonder why you were cut short by a fat woman with a trolley full of grocery at the department store that evening. The inner babble tells you that you look timid and easy to push around. Then you think of all the situations and dialogues with friends and colleagues where and when you were passed over for someone else for a promotion or pushed around. By the time, your dinner is ready to be laid on the table, you are feeling depressed and feel terrible over the fact that you have allowed yourself to be treated like a doormat.

Suddenly you realise that your partner could have offered help with kitchen work instead of surfing the net. You are convinced that this is another situation where you are being taken for granted by him. Unfortunately one moment leads to another and you snap at him over dinner creating a tense atmosphere with the children wondering if they are at fault too. Sounds familiar?

Most of us go through incessant negative chatter. The effects of this chatter are serious and deeply affect our thoughts, actions and behavior and it is a habit that is not easy to outgrow. Fortunately there are a few things you can do about this nuisance to help you develop a calm and focused mind, one with positive thoughts that will boost your personality and self-esteem.

In the pages that follow, I have chalked out some cues on what you could do to stop the nuisance of negation and be your own best friend. I have also given pointers on situations you should avoid at times when you feel vulnerable to negative self-banter until you make a recovery.

Mentor Your Mind

Tips to defend yourself against self deprecation:

- ✓ Immediately note the depth and pace of your breathing. It will be a shallow breath (air inhaled only up to your throat) and moderate to rapid in pace.
- ✓ Be aware of what your mind is babbling.

- ✓ Watch the thoughts just as an outsider would. Detach yourself from the thoughts by assuming an observer posture.
- ✓ Once your self-observation process is over (this will take no more than 30 seconds), forcefully and at once change the direction of your thoughts.
- ✓ You can do this by talking to someone in the house or office about something else which has no negative content in it.
- ✓ Alternatively, if you are alone, you can force yourself a positive thought such as "I am blessed to not go hungry tonight" or "I am lucky to have a home to return to."
- ✓ Have your workstation area at home or office, kitchen and most importantly the most observed part of your bedroom filled with positive thoughts, sayings, prayers etc. – those that make you realise what you have instead of what you do not.
- ✓ Every morning before you leave for office, and after you return from work, take 2 minutes of your time and stand in front of a mirror (preferably a full length mirror, but any mirror that reflects your face fully will also suffice). Look into the eyes of your image and tell yourself audibly "I am God's child and so I am perfect." You can also say "I love myself" or "I forgive myself." Repeat this sentence at least 20 times.
- ✓ You should stay with one statement for at least a week. Analyse what negativity about yourself you need to address most and then affirm positivity of the same element.
- ✓ Your statement should be spoken out audibly and slowly. It should reach the ears of your mind.
- ✓ Write a diary at the end of the day. Include in it your efforts towards infusing positivity in your life and thoughts.

- ✓ Include how you kept out negativity today.
- ✓ Also write if you were successful at your attempts and those that took time. The ones that took time to push out are the ones you need to affirm in front of the mirror for longer time period.
- ✓ Listen to calming instrumental music as much as you can in the day – while dressing, while driving, while cooking etc.
- ✓ Develop a hobby, go for walks etc.
- ✓ Above all, stay in tune and aware of your breathing patterns at times when negativity strikes and correct it immediately restoring deep, slow and calm breathing.

Situations, Thoughts, Actions and People To Keep Away From At Such Times:

- Do not surround yourself with people who back-bite and talk behind others' back.
- Keep away from those who are all negative about the world around them. Being in the company of people driven by negativity drains substantial mental and emotional energy from a person and leaves you feeling tired and low.
- Avoid watching television or reading the newspaper as a first activity in the morning or the last activity before bedtime at night.
- The media's business is to attract readership/viewership and increase their TRPs. Good news does not make for attractive pieces and so they keep at bad news and sensationalizing.
- In your bid to welcome positivity in your life, be aware that you are not becoming oblivious to the real and actual sufferings of the people around you and the world in general.
- Suffering exists. Know that, but choose to push positivity in your life.

- Do not put off healthy eating, practice of self-defence techniques against negativity and staying active with workouts and hobbies.
- Healthy living promotes healthy thoughts and vice versa.
- Stay away from (be aware of) the blame- guilt-grudge trap.
- Stop measuring everything in extreme terms and generalising the behaviours and patterns on others and yourself.
- Watch when you are starting to label yourself and often on how the others perceive you.
- Stay away from attitudes in life and media that promote perfection in work, home and play.
- There is no set or perfect way to live your life. Everyone chalks their own destiny to suit their unique situations.
- Keep away from colleagues at office and friends who make you feel inferior while you are in the process of working on your self-deprecation habit.
- Consciously keep the consumption of alcohol, nicotine, caffeine to the minimum while you are working at your self-negation habits. Any substance that makes you step up your breathing and heart rate is avoidable during this time.

Remember my stress is always on consistency. There is no magic way except to keep at the techniques. Negation is a potent destructive weapon which we unknowingly cultivate at our hands. It strengthens our negative attitude to life and eventually affects our judgments and performance. Because it is a self-destructive practice, it needs perseverance in warding off. Do not expect drastic results within a week. However, you will start to notice the little changes in your thought patterns within this period of time.

4. The pressure of parental care

Your ageing or ailing parent needs looking after. S/he and you decide mutually that they move in with you. Whatever the reason (you could be the only child or the child they are most comfortable with), you take on the responsibility and decide to roll with the punches. However after the 'honeymoon' of the first week is over, your life begins to show signs of complications and stress. Your spouse/partner and children feel neglected and though you seem to be running around trying to cater to everyone's emotional and other needs, your parent also begins to exhibit difficult behaviour. As weeks slip past, you notice that:

- You feel tired and stressed most of the time having frequent headaches and stomach upsets.
- You are often wrought with feelings of guilt and resentment.
- You wish for days of privacy and non-interference.
- You lose appetite and much of your restful sleep.
- You seem to be experiencing what seems like mood swings and depression.
- Your work place behaviour becomes erratic.
- You become withdrawn from your social circle.

If you are experiencing any or few of these emotions, you are bearing the burden of parental care instead of enjoying their limited time. And though it is easier said than done, life could become a very tight rope walk, balancing too many variables and seem like fighting a losing battle.

This is not how you had planned it. Or had you planned it at all? However, there are a few things you can still put into place that could reduce some amount of mental stress and bring more order into your mood and routine. Once you get the routine in flow, you should be able to reap the benefits of an elder in the house.

Positive Psychology: Weapon against the sinister six 35

I have provided a ballpark schedule. You are free to change the times given to suit your convenience. Also, you do not have to fit in everything that has been suggested into the same day. You can choose to leave any 2 activities on a given day but make sure you follow them up the next day. I have given a broad timetable for the weekend so that your first days into the working week do not come across as heavy.

Day	Pre-Breakfast	Post-Breakfast	Pre-Lunch	Post-Lunch	Around Tea	Pre-Dinner
SAT & SUN	Chalk out the weekend chores like laundry, grocery etc. and who's to do them	Take care of parent's needs – doctor's visit, medicines, bathing, clothes darning, talk to them about them	With children – homework help, playtime, talk to them	With Spouse / partner – couple grocery with coffee, talk to him about him and you, go for a walk	Speak to a friend on phone, go visiting, take time out yourself*	Get the whole family together to do something – watch TV movie, just sit and read, games, cooking, etc.

When I mentioned taking time out for you in the column captioned 'Around Tea', I meant to bring focus on to yourself. You will be the pillar who has the house functioning, on who almost all members of the family depend for food, emotional support etc. You need to be healthy above anything else and more than anyone else deserves to be! Imagine you sick or unhappy in such a set-up. The foundations of the house will begin to rock in no time. Here is how you can help yourself and in the process reduce your anxieties and mood swings, your feeling of guilt and resentment:

1. Take care of your physical fitness first.
    a. Include time for any workout -a walk, run or jog, swimming, etc.

b. Eat healthy, small portions and more frequently.
   c. Learn relaxation techniques.
   d. Do indulge in sweet treats but no more than twice a week.
2. Set a fixed time to go to bed every night, say at 9 pm.
3. It is essential you maintain your social network.
   a. You may not be as active, but make sure you are talking to at least 2 friends every week or visiting another every other week or even having them over.
4. Planning will be an integral part of life so when you plan to go for that movie or take that vacation, speak with the parent as well.
   a. Assure them that they will be looked after till you are back.
   b. Ask them if they would want to take the time to visit elsewhere.
   c. Tell them of the help you are getting at home for him/her while they are away.
5. Take time out for yourself:
   a. Seek that hairdresser's appointment.
   b. Get yourself a massage done.
   c. Indulge in treating yourself to good foods once a week or a new outfit once a month.

Not the least, you must remember at all times that:

- Your parents raised you in the best way they knew and pampered you swhen they could.
- It is perfectly normal to seek help of support groups if you find the going difficult the first few months – such as those of local area agencies for the aged, support organizations that deal with depression or stress.
- It is not right to push your body beyond its limits to accomplish all on your To-do list. You need to prioritise, plan, delegate and team-up.

- Your ticking all activities chalked for the day is not necessarily a reflection of who you are or your worth.

With these pointers it will be easy for you to chart out your life at least broadly so that you will experience less worry and anxiety in everyday living with a live-in parent.

5. The stressful saga of socializing

After much indecision about that special someone, you finally settle on a person you are sure you want to spend your life with. Your new partner has a moderately-sized social circle of his own. He asks you out on a weekend lunch with his friends and their partners. You freeze at the suggestion though you have wanted to go out with him all week. You say you are unsure of your plans and seem upset. He wonders if he has said something wrong and seems tense and worse, apologetic. He thought he was doing the right thing by introducing you to his friends as a mark of your relationship having moved up a notch on the commitment scale. Meanwhile, you go through the following emotions:

- Fearful of his company's evaluation and acceptance of you.
- Scared that the others will notice your nervousness.
- Anxious that you may act in a way that will embarrass you and him.
- You experience nausea and dizziness along with muscle stiffness and a trembling voice.
- You feel your heart race or sink and you get hot flashes not to mention sweaty palms when you think about it at night.
- You lose sleep worrying excessively over the meeting and think of excuses you can make to avoid the situation.
- Continuing to predict the worst possible outcomes during and after the 'meet', you are barely able to

focus on anything else in your life till you resolve the situation to either fight or flee.

If this is what you go through every time you receive a friend's or colleague's invite to an outing, then you are not alone. It is estimated that approximately 15 million American adults (6.8% of total population in age bracket of over 18 years in any given year) suffer from social phobia.[9] The condition generally begins around the age of 13.[10]

However, there is hope. The road to hope is a rough one but it gets easier each time you go through it until you start to enjoy the process! Yes, a sizeable percentage of those suffering from this disorder get treated just following the cognitive behavioural path not always accompanied by medication.

I have chalked out a progression of actions you can follow in sequence before you go out to meet someone and when you are there at the venue to make you feel calmer and one which will eventually help you look forward to such socializing.

Each time you are predicting the worst outcomes of a meet-up, getting entangled in labelling yourself and worrying what others think of you all the time while you highlight your own negatives and compare yourself unfavourably to others spiralling down to more anxiety and dread, you can follow the steps that mentor your mind into self-control.

Mentor Your Mind

At home:

1. Do not be in a rush to respond to the invite. Let them know you will be there at the last day. However, do not use this as an excuse to wriggle out of the invitation.

---

9. Kessler RC, Chiu WT, Demler O, Walters EE. Prevalence, severity, and co morbidity of twelve-month DSM-IV disorders in the National Co morbidity Survey Replication (NCS-R). *Archives of General Psychiatry*, 2005 June; 62(6):617-27.

10. Kessler RC, Berglund PA, Demler O, Jin R, Walters EE. Lifetime prevalence and age-of-onset distributions of DSM-IV disorders in the National Co morbidity Survey Replication (NCS-R). Archives of General Psychiatry. 2005 June; 62(6):593-602.

2. Take out a diary and put down all your fears.
3. Challenge each of the fears in writing first with logical thought inputs and then read them out loud.
4. Next sit down on the floor in lotus posture or any posture you are comfortable in. Follow the sequence that depicts a powerful yoga exercise:
   a. Close your eyes and breathe in. Imagine fresh, cool energising air getting into you. Mentally count to 4 as you inhale slowly and deeply.
   b. Hold on to the inhaled breath for 2 seconds.
   c. Exhale to a mental count of 6 – slow and easy. This is known as the 'Nadi-Shoddhan' Pranayama. It will take the edge off the stress and with repetitions diminish your physical symptoms of anxiety such as clammy hands, racing heart and trembling voice etc.
   d. Repeat steps a-c for five full minutes.
   e. Slowly open your eyes and audibly tell yourself, "I am perfectly capable of handling any situation. I will be fine. I will enjoy myself at the party."
5. Whenever you encounter the physical symptoms later again, you can use any of the above-mentioned techniques or use positive visualization repetitively to gain confidence and look forward to the event. Here is a sample technique[11]:
   a. Write down all the positive suggestions you want to make to yourself during the meditative state on a piece of paper. Suggestion should be written in positive and active voice and in the present tense. You may take help from a certified professional or the internet available licensed resources in the writing of suggestions.
   b. Read it a couple of times so that you know what to suggest to yourself.

---

11. Migraines For The Informed Woman. Author: Mamta Singh. Publisher: Rupa & Co. Page(s): 83-86. ISBN: 9788129115171. First Edition.

c. Block out external noises with very soft instrumental music of your choice (CDs and tapes specific in pre-hypnosis music are available nowadays).
d. Sit on a mat on an even floor.
e. Close your eyes softly.
f. Take a deep breath and let go (exhale). Repeat once more.
g. Take your attention (with closed eyes) to your head (skull). Tell yourself that the muscles in your head are relaxing and that they are not stressed, taut or tense. Breathe in slow and deep. Breathe out slow and full. Continue to be in the head zone till the time you feel that the cranium is relaxed and eased.
h. Move to the forehead. Repeat the same process – tell yourself to let go of tight forehead muscles and eyebrows. While doing this breathe in and out slowly and fully.
i. Continue down to the other parts of the body – eyes, nose, lips, tongue, cheeks, chin, neck, shoulders, arms, palms, fingers, chest, abdomen, thighs (quadriceps, hamstrings and piriformis), knees, shin, calves, ankle, feet and toes.
j. Take a little bit longer in body parts you feel need more time to relax. Do not hurry this process. Breathe in and out slowly and completely while relaxing the body parts.
k. Transport yourself mentally to your favourite place in the world – a place where you feel free of stress, safe and secure.
l. Stay here for a minute or two imagining doing whatever it is you liked doing in this place.
m. If your thoughts begin to waver, bring yourself back to this place.
n. Start your suggestions to yourself by speaking out slowly and clearly.

o. Wait for approximately 15 seconds and repeat the suggestion slowly and clearly.
p. The more you repeat the stronger the faith becomes in it.
q. After you are done, wait for 30 seconds for the messages and process to sink in and calm to build in.
r. Awaken yourself by telling that you are arising out of trance at Count #1. Tell yourself you have washed your face with cool stream water at Count #2 and that you are now fresh to start the day with new energy and beliefs at Count #3.
s. Slowly open your eyes.
t. Stay in this position for 15 seconds before you get up to go.

Support Activities:

a. Join classes on improving behavioural skills in social set-ups.
b. Learn to be more assertive.
c. Learn more relaxation techniques. These could be physical or emotional techniques as well. They could draw from Yoga or meditation or physical exercises.
d. Make a list of things you fear. Start working on each fear from the last fear listed upwards. As you work up the fear ladder, celebrate and reinforce after victory over each fear. Break the huge task into small bits. Record the feelings in your diary.

Remember at all times that:

1. The climb back requires courage and patience.
2. Take small steps at a time to chip away at the fear block.
3. Picture yourself as having fun and enjoying every minute of the get-together.
4. Know that almost everyone there at the group will be nervous to varying degrees to begin with. You are not alone.

5. Stay outwardly focussed. Talk to people. Ask about them. Turn the tables, so it seems that you are evaluating them instead.

6. The woes of weight

You are at a mall shopping for a dress that will be perfect for the after-hour office party or for a friend's house-warming invite. You almost know what you want. At the mall, you rummage through five large clothes stores before you finally spot exactly what you had in mind. After a moment's deliberation, you settle for what would not have been your first choice but acceptable for the occasion. You try on the outfit and then turn to the mirror in the trial room. It looks good save for the bulge on your waist that shows in the cut of this dress. You feel depressed and go to the host's party wearing what you think suits you best but one that they have seen you many times in. All through the party, you are conscious of this fact and your unease is not allayed by the fact that quite a few friends and colleagues have new dresses on and look fabulous in them. Suddenly, you feel unattractive and worthless, slipping towards low self-esteem. Do you suppose you have been through this situation?

I want you to do a fact check today. Starting now, keep track of the number of exposures you get about the rightness of being slim, thin, fit through the day. Count all the print media, electronic media (TV and the internet) and advertisement on hoardings. Include all the talks and expressions of people you come across with similar insinuations about food, diets, calories etc. What does it say? Yes, the weight obsession in people is a little more serious and of epic proportions than the issue of being overweight or obese.

Keeping this in mind, my previous book, The Urban Woman's Integrated Fitness Guide did not focus on obesity and overweight issues. The focus rather was how to keep active, which workouts to do etc. thus bringing about bodily change as a side-effect as opposed to the direct reason for keeping and staying active.

To be able to gauge whether you are overweight or falsely hold that perspective, here's the Body Mass Index (BMI) method to enable quick and ready diagnosis. I say 'quick and ready' because it is not a precise indicator of your weight condition.

$$BMI = \frac{\text{Your Weight in Kilograms (or pounds)}}{\text{Your Height in centimetres (or feet and inches)}}$$

If the value is a number > 25 but below 30, you are said to be overweight. For values of 30 and above, you are indicated as obese[12].

You can clearly see the flaw in this pointer and yet the media speaks of little else besides BMI. Today Waist-Hip-Ratio, Recovery Heart Rate etc. are used as more precise indicators of good health. BMI will tell you

- You are fat if you are big-boned or muscular.
- You are underweight, if you are in the older age group and have experienced loss of muscle tone.

Without losing total perspective, an overweight reading as per the BMI will by and large indicate if you are likely to suffer from diseases concerning weight issues later in life. Quoting from Obesity: Preventing and Managing the Global Epidemic – A Report of a WHO Consultation (WHO Technical Report Series 894), "Overweight and obesity represent a rapidly growing threat to the health of populations in an increasing number of countries. Indeed they are now so common that they are replacing more traditional problems such as under-nutrition and infectious

---

12. Overweight and obesity are defined as abnormal or excessive fat accumulation that presents a risk to health. A crude population measure of obesity is the body mass index (BMI), a person's weight (in kilograms) divided by the square of his or her height (in metres). A person with a BMI of 30 or more is generally considered obese. A person with a BMI equal to or more than 25 is considered overweight. "Dietary And Socio-Economic Factors Associated with Obesity in North Indian Population" - A report by Neetu Gupta (Department of Home Science, Kurukshetra University) published in ISPUB. The Internet Journal Of Health. Vol 9.Issn:1528-8315

diseases as the most significant causes of ill-health. Obesity co-morbidities include coronary heart disease, hypertension and stroke, certain types of cancer, non-insulin-dependent diabetes mellitus, gallbladder disease, dyslipidaemia, osteoarthritis and gout, and pulmonary diseases, including sleep apnoea. In addition, the obese suffer from social bias, prejudice and discrimination, on the part not only of the general public but also of health professionals, and this may make them reluctant to seek medical assistance."[13]

Mentor Your Mind

It is important that you understand that you may not be totally in control and thus responsible for your weight condition. Realise that an increase in your weight may have occurred due to any of the following factors:

- Malfunctioning thyroid glands.
- Genetic disposition towards weight gain or body fat.
- Taking of certain prescription drugs which have weight gain listed as a possible side-effect.
- Stress

However, it is even more critical to be very aware if your state of being overweight or obese has been brought about by factors that are in your control such as:

- Leading a sedentary life.
- Binge eating.
- Eating inappropriate types of foods.
- Lack of sleep.
- Frequent dieting.

As with all the other conditions, I have put together a timetable for you that takes into consideration your busy day and yet integrates self-discipline that will put you on the path to healthy eating and living.

---

13. Obesity: preventing and managing the global epidemic. Author: World Health Organization. Published in 2000. ISBN: 9241208945.

Time	What to Eat or Do	Comment
5:30 am	• Light tea or coffee with 1 cube of sugar.	• Make this light on caffeine. • Caffeine hinders the break down and absorption of vitamins and minerals till 40 minutes after intake. • If you wish to have strong tea or coffee, precede it with a mug of water.
6 -6:20 am	• Brisk walk to work up mild to moderate sweat.	• Preferably out in open air or inside home/apartment.
6:30 am	• 1 Banana • Low fat yoghurt without sugar.	• Banana helps curb acidity or sensitive morning stomachs with a pH value of 4.8.
8:30 am	• 1 Sunny side up egg/omelette or 1 serving* of moog sprouts. • 1 washed apple with skin on.	• You can take this as a part of your snack packed from home. • You can take any other fruit of choice if apple is not an option on a given day.
10:30 am	• 1 Low fat cheese or chutney sandwich. • 1 serving* of any vegetable or fruit salad.	• You can take this as a part of your snack packed from home.
12:30 am	• 1 cup of lentil soup • 2 Brown bread sandwiches or 2 chapattis. • 1 serving* of chicken or fish done in minimal oil (preferably steamed or grilled or sautéed). • 1 serving of any cooked vegetable or an equal amount of salad.	• This is your lunch • Include as many colours in your salad – beet, carrot, lettuce, tomato, boiled corn, etc.

Time	What to Eat or Do	Comment
3 pm	• 1 cup of Yoghurt • 5 each of almonds and walnuts	• Flavoured yoghurts will do as long as they are low in fat.
5 – 5:30 pm	• 1 cup of light coffee or tea with 1 cube of sugar. • or 1 light latte	
6 – 6:30 pm	• Go running or jogging	• This is your workout time. Please do not substitute this time for running groceries or checking emails. • If you cannot run or jog, do some circuit training. • Yoga and Pranayama are good options. • A rough indicator of a good session is heart rate going up to 135 bpm and sweating.
7 pm	• 1 serving* Cottage cheese/paneer dish cooked in minimum oil. • A pair of chicken or fish sandwich or 2 chapattis. • 1 serving* of lentil soup or *daal*. • 1 serving* of sautéed vegetables.	• This is your dinner. • If you want to substitute the chapatti with rice, you should use 2 servings of brown rice instead.
8- 8:15 pm	• Reflect on the day. • Lovingly stroke your stomach or any other part of the body you feel is 'fat' indicating acceptance and unconditional love. • Closing your eyes and sitting on the floor, audibly repeat to yourself: "I am fit and healthy."	• These positive affirmations are as important as the process of healthy eating and exercises.

Time	What to Eat or Do	Comment
	• "My body has got all that it needs today." • "I love my body. I love myself."	• They work at a subconscious level and bring about results beyond our comprehension. • Focus on your affirmations while you are doing them.

***Note:** Serving sizes of specific foods can be had from http://web.mit.edu/athletics/sportsmedicine/wcrservings.html - Massachusetts Inst of Tech. - *MIT Sports Medicine*

Take another look at the chart. How do you benefit from it?

1. You have approached weight via the diet, exercise and emotional route incorporating balanced foods, elimination of toxics and junk foods, activity and right thoughts.
2. The foods that you are to eat for lunch or dinner need minimal cooking time and can be prepared the evening before or even fixed in a hurry in the morning.
3. They do not require excessive planning or exotic ingredients.
4. I have provided alternatives, so that if you are bored with one dish, you may replace it with a similar option.
5. Adhering to this routine does not leave you hungry through the day as most diets do, making you crave ever more for high sugar foods. You are eating 9 times in the day and will still see results!

Meditation: Tune in and out at will

In a very rudimentary sense, meditation is the process of attaining and remaining in the mindfulness of the 'now' or the present moment. It is a holistic discipline with roots in all religions. With the practice of the process of self-regulation of thoughts and attention, it is possible to achieve a relaxed and peaceful mind and a higher state of consciousness, improved concentration not to mention provide the body with immense other benefits (especially to the cardiovascular, respiratory, circulatory, digestive and endocrine systems). Meditation has been seen to bring about physical and biochemical changes within. It has also been used by researchers in clinical settings to manage stress and pain reduction.

Meditation is practiced by people for two most popular reasons – to de-stress and to improve their attention or focus. I have provided a sample meditation for both the requirements. It must be kept in mind that the meditation technique is only one among the various methods or way to achieve the goal stated. You may use variants to suit your need. It is also best to initiate yourself into meditation under a certified Yoga instructor or Meditation expert. As with any discipline, the magic of benefits is in your consistency with them.

Meditation: Tune in and out at will

Meditation for relaxation

Posture:
1. Sit on a mat on an even floor.
2. You can use the Lotus posture or the Cross-Legged posture to sit comfortably.
3. Rest your palms on your knees, facing upwards towards the sky or ceiling.
4. Adjust yourself on the mat so that your hips are well balanced without you leaning on to any one side more or putting weight on any one.
5. Push your belly out a little and sit back allowing for an erect posture. The spine should be erect yet comfortable.
6. Your shoulders should be relaxed.
7. You may drop your head a little so that the chin is closer to the throat to relax the facial muscles.
8. Relax your eyes as you close them instead of shutting them tight.

Meditation:
1. Bring your attention to your breathing.
2. With every inhalation, think: Every breath coming into me brings energy and cool freshness.
3. With every exhalation, think: Every breath leaving me relaxes me, taking with it tensions of my body and my mind.
4. Stay with this thought for 30 seconds.
5. Observe your breathing just as an outsider would.
6. Follow the breath in – from the tip of your nose, through the nasal passage, down the wind pipe and filling your lung.
7. Follow the breath out – from the lung back to the nasal passage and out.

8. Stay with this breath following process for another 30 seconds.
9. You may realise your mind is wondering amid this process and other thoughts are interfering.
10. The moment you notice the interference, return to your breathing. (Steps 2-7)
11. Meditate in this way for 10 minutes.

As you master this relaxation meditation with time, you may add to it what is also known as body relaxation. After following through till Step 8, given above, you can start to think of each part of your body beginning from your feet, up to your head, including your calves, thighs, hips, back, abdomen, shoulders, chest, neck, face, tongue as you go. Think of each of these body parts one at a time for 30 seconds and remain with the thought that it is relaxing, letting go of tension and leaving its weight on to the floor.

The combined meditation can be made to last up to 20 minutes.

Meditation for improving focus

Posture:

1. Choose a room where no direct draught of air (natural, fan, air cooler, air conditioner, blower etc.) hits you or an area of 2 feet around you. I specify this so that the draught does not cause a flutter or movement in the object you will choose to concentrate on.
2. Place any one object of small or medium size at an easy distance of 2 feet from you. It could be a natural item such as a single tone/hue flower, an apple or a burning/lit candle.
3. Sit on a mat on an even floor.
4. You can use the Lotus posture or the Cross-Legged posture to sit comfortably.
5. Rest your palms on your knees, facing upwards towards the sky or ceiling.

Meditation: Tune in and out at will

6. Adjust yourself on the mat so that your hips are well balanced without you leaning on to any one side more or putting weight on any one.
7. Push your belly out a little and sit back allowing for an erect posture. The spine should be erect yet comfortable.
8. Your shoulders should be relaxed.
9. Still your body.

Meditation:
1. Take a few deep breaths in and out and settle into a comfortable breathing rhythm.
2. Take your attention to the object you have selected and placed straight in front of you.
3. Look at it for 5 seconds, eyes relaxed, unstrained and unsquinting.
4. If thoughts interfere after a while, bring your focus back to the object you have placed.
5. When the rate of blinking reduces after 2-3 minutes and you enter a staring mode, you can close your eyes to relax it.
6. When you close your eyes, an afterimage of the object you have been looking at will form and appear in the middle of your two eyebrows. Concentrate on this image. Look at this image with your internal eye.
7. When the image disappears, you may open your eyes again to look at the object you placed in front of you
8. Continue doing so for 5 minutes.

With the passage of time, you will be able to increase the length of this meditation and also observe that you are able to think deeper about the object you are seeing than just its external appearance such as its texture, flavour, content, cells, pigments, taste, colour, aroma etc. You will be able to go deeper into the object.

As oft repeated in this book, results of any process mentioned (meditations included) can be had with patient practice, consistency and regularity.

Physical Exercises to Stub Stress

Just as meditation, relaxation techniques, Yoga, Positive affirmations, Pranayama etc. help in rapid and effective control of stress and stress symptoms, physical exercises and workouts have also proved to have an immediate effect towards stress reduction.

Any exercise induces the body's pituitary gland to release endorphins. There are 4 different types of endorphins – alpha, beta, gamma and sigma. It is found that during prolonged exercise sessions, acidosis of the blood occurs, which is indicated by decrease in the blood flow and oxygen to the muscle tissues. This triggers the release of beta-endorphins, as a response to tackle the anticipated pain or stress. These beta-endorphins have analgesic properties and raise the bar for the body in tackling any bodily pains.

Similarly, another polypeptide, the enkephalin, is released by the thalamus of the brain during periods of exercise. They have the specific capacity to block the neurotransmitter, Substance P, which is notorious in triggering migraines.

Catecholamines are another substance, which is released in short periods of exerting exercises. They raise the density and secretion of serotonin mildly and help counter bodily pains and stress to some extent.

The benefits from any exercise routine are immense. It helps clear the toxins accumulated in the tissues involving pain, strengthens neck and back muscles which are effected in migraines and other body pain conditions such as neuralgia etc., improves cardiovascular condition, improves endurance, flexibility and increases overall body strength, increases endorphin levels in general in the body to help tackle pain, helps alleviate bad mood and depressions with increasing the level of serotonin release. It also boosts confidence through a healthy lifestyle and fosters a feeling of gaining control over your life choices.

You will do good to choose any sport or aerobic activity which you enjoy, are interested in and are comfortable with such as Step aerobics, martial arts, skipping, swimming, squash, tennis, badminton, trekking, football, basketball, Pilates, yoga, gardening, biking, jogging, running, dancing, skiing, strength training etc. However, over the years I have found interval training suits best as a stress buster. Any high intensity cardiovascular activity which makes your heart beat at approximately 80-85% of its maximum permissible heart rate will cause the body to release endorphin (or the feel good hormone). Interval training also suits fat burning best.

Below, I have used the interval exercise I designed for my book, The Urban Woman's Integrated Fitness Guide. Please get a doctor's clearance before you attempt this exercise.

On the run - intermediate level treadmill workout with built-in intervals:

Total Duration = 30 minutes

Phase	Comments	*Duration (Min)	*Speed (Miles Per Hour)	Incline	% of Max Heart Rate*
Warm Up	Brisk Walk	5	3.5 – 4	0%	50%-60%
Workout	Jog	3	4.25 – 4.5	0.5%	65%-70%
Workout	Run	1	4.7	0%	70%-75%
Workout	Jog	5	4.25 - 4.5	1%	70%-75%
Workout	Sprint	1	4.9 - 5.3	0%	75% - 85%

Physical Exercises to Stub Stress 55

Workout	Jog	10	4.25 – 4.5	0%	65%-70%
Cool Down	Walk	5	3.75	0%	50%-60%

*The table contains indicative values only. You must adjust your values on the treadmill as per your height, fitness levels, body signals, etc. in the duration of the exercise. Miles per hour (mph) values may be converted to Kilometres per hour (kmph) values by multiplying mph by 1.6.

The 30-minute jogging for a 150 lbs (approximately 68 kg) person at the above-mentioned speed and incline will burn close to 280 calories in half an hour.

It is important that you keep track of the %MHR[12] reading that your treadmill measures for you during your workout. For the intermediate level exercisers, the goal should be to remain in the 70% - 80% intensity level. If values exceed this reading on your treadmill, it is advisable that you slow down and readjust your speed, incline and thus the intensity of your workout.

It is important to note that you do your warm up and cool down sections built into the workouts. It may happen that you launch straight into the workout section without the requisite warm up for the stipulated duration. This may give high %MHR readings. As with the beginners, you must stay with this workout routine for a period of 12 weeks, working out thrice a week, before you attempt any workout in the advanced category.

CAUTION!

If you are not particularly energetic on any scheduled workout day, you must do your workout at an easy pace and intensity level, such as at the beginner's level or slower (just walking on the treadmill) and as per your comfort level. It is not recommended that you set ambitious targets for yourself day-on-day at this stage without respecting body signals. Similarly, move on to the next level of advanced training only

---

14. Maximum Heart Rate or MHR = 220-Age.

if you are confident of yourself. Individuals are unique as is their physicality. You will be your best guide in the progress of your regimen. At this point, I would also encourage you to talk to your gym instructor and get more hands on help with your posture and real time needs while working out. You could also join fitness groups in your locality or on the internet to discuss fitness issues specific to you.

Take a ride – intermediate level stationary bike workout with built-in intervals

Total Duration = 30 minutes

Phase	Comments	*Duration (Min)	*Speed (Miles Per Hour)	Resistance	% of Max Heart Rate*
Warm Up	Manual	5	10	3	50% - 60%
Workout	Aerobics	3	12 - 15	3	65% - 70%
Workout	Fat Burner	1	12	5	70% - 75%
Workout	Aerobics	5	15 – 18	3	70% - 75%
Workout	Fat Burner	1	10	7	75% - 80%
Workout	Aerobics	10	15 – 18	3	65% - 70%
Cooling	Manual	5	10	2	50% - 60%

*The table contains indicative values only. You must adjust your values on the treadmill as per your height, fitness levels, body signals, etc. in the duration of the exercise. Miles per hour (mph) values may be converted to Kilometres per hour (kmph) values by multiplying mph by 1.6.

It is important that you keep track of the %MHR reading that your stationary bike measures for you during your workout. For the intermediate-level exercisers, the goal should be to remain in the 70% - 80% intensity level. If values exceed this reading on your stationary bike at any given point during your session, it is advisable that you slow down and readjust your speed and intensity (resistance level) of your workout. In case you feel the need to rest, you should take the time to recover, whatever that period of time is, before you resume your session. Your body will be the best real-time judge in all your workout sessions, so it is important that you do not get distracted with television watching or MP3 etc. at your gym or home at the time of your workout.

As you get fitter and feel calmer after your workout, you may increase either the duration, speed or the resistance levels in your workout or any combination thereof. This in effect will mean that you have moved to the next level – the advanced level of training.

You may also want to combine a lower intensity stationary bike workout with some weight training. Mild to moderate strength training may be done after your stationary bike workout. This will step up your ability to burn fats more readily. The fat burning graph will continue to show a spiked but steady rate with weights as the activity involves low impact at a low pace. This will also increase your endurance capacity.

However, if you feel you are not ready to combine the two yet, you must continue with only the bike workout until you feel fit, strong, less tired and experience more peace and contentment post exercise, to try and mix the two in a single workout session.

A 30-minute biking session for a 150 lbs (approximately 68 kg) person at the above-mentioned speed and intensity will burn close to 250 calories in half an hour.

Other roads to mental fitness

As with most ailments, there is more than a single path to obtain relief. A single option or a combination of any two, if adhered to for a reasonable period of time, and with persistence, will generally yield the desired result. Here's a brief outline of the options and what they entail:

Option	Comment
1. Meditation	A self regulatory, holistic process which can reduce arousal state and hyperactive autonomic system response by taking the mind to deeper states of relaxation and awareness.
2. Bio-feedback	A process utilising sensing and detecting gadgets to make a person aware of their physiological functions such as brainwaves, pain sensing, heart rate, body temperature, etc., so that it's manipulation is easy at will to improve thoughts, emotions, behaviour and overall health.
3. Pranayama	An Ayurvedic technique of regulation and control of life breath which researches show helps in treating a range of stress related disorders, improving autonomic functions, reducing signs of oxidative stress. It claims to develop a steady mind, strong will-power, and emotional stability by enhancing perception.
4. Psychotherapy	<u>Cognitive Behaviour Therapy</u>: This focuses on identifying dysfunctional emotions, negative thoughts, irrational beliefs and thought patterns and then challenging them through a systematic and scientific procedure. <u>Graded Exposure Therapy</u>: Here you confront your fears starting with the least fearful to what you consider the scariest, in a safe, controlled environment. Through repeated exposures, either in your imagination or in reality, to the feared object or situation, you gain a greater sense of control eventually causing your anxieties and stress to disappear. <u>Talk Therapy</u>: The clinical psychologist takes you through your experience and talks to you logically through it and out of it and also provides counselling.
5. Acupuncture	A traditional Chinese line of treatment wherein filiform needles are inserted and manipulated at specific points on the body surface where it believes Qi flows to correct a wide range of physical, mental and emotional imbalances such as anxiety, phobia, pain, weight loss, depression, OCD, etc.

Option	Comment
6. Hypnosis	A mental state that is brought about by the process of a long series of preliminary instructions and suggestions where the person enters into a wakeful state of focused attention and heightened suggestibility. Often used in psychotherapy to treat depression, sleep and anxiety disorders, Phobia, OCD, PTSD and anorexia conditions.
7. Massage and Reflexology	Massage is a procedure of applying pressure to different parts of the body using pummelling, kneading, cupping etc. techniques to relax the body and Reflexology also involves application of pressure but chiefly to the feet to address various health conditions.
8. Aromatherapy	A holistic line of treatment using volatile plant compounds to alter a person's mood, health and cognitive function through stimulation of glands and release of required hormones.

You must remember that each of these lines of treatment is a science by itself and would not see justice within the confines of this book. If you wish to go deeper into the subject matter, practice and tenets of these sciences, it will be advisable you seek a licensed professional of the field and learn from authentically certified experts. However, for those long term victims or for those who exhibit acute symptoms, these methods can be used as supplementing the medication path.

How Can You Tell it's Time to See a Doctor

Answering your questions

Seeing a doctor at the first signs of mental stress or feeling anxious about a situation is neither desirable nor necessary. It is alright to feel tense in some circumstances we are faced with in our lives. Our biological systems are gifted with the complex neuro-endocrine system which controls our nervous response.

Amongst the various glands of the endocrine system, the pituitary gland is considered the master gland and is located in the front lower end of the temporal lobes of our brain. Among other functions, it signals adrenal glands when to release adrenaline (or epinephrine) and noradrenalin (norepinephrine) that have helped us survive as a species. These hormones raise our body temperature, heart beats, force of contraction apart from blood sugar levels and fatty acid concentration in our blood. They also constrict arteries from areas not required for an immediate nervous and physical response to a given situation the mind perceives as a threat. If we had no internal alarm systems to go off, to tell us to fight or flee, we would have been wiped out in the evolutionary scheme of things.

So if nervous responses were considered normal, as it were,

How Can You Tell it's Time to See a Doctor

- Should we ever consider consulting a doctor for conditions of anxiety, depression, mood swings, loss of focus and other such?
- And if we do need to see a doctor, how should we know when to see one?
- And more importantly, why is it then necessary to follow the advice given in this book or any other? Why not see a doctor for medication to start with and cut short our rough ride?

The prudent answer to if we need to consult a doctor or psychologist or a psychiatrist is 'Yes'. The more important is to know when it's time to see one or what the signs are that tell us it's time for a consultation. See if you tick/check more than five out of the ten questions given below in the checklist. If yes, it is an indication to seek professional help.

1. You have been suffering with your mental discomfort for more than 6 months continually.
2. Your condition has affected your sleep – both quality and quantity for over 2 months now despite trying methods to get into your original sleep pattern.
3. Your discomfort has had a negative impact in your eating habits – overeating/binge eating leading to abnormal weight gain or showing signs of anorexia leading to unusual weight loss.
4. It is an ordeal to get to work or make presentations or sit through a meeting.
5. You experience palpitations and the feeling of 'sinking' heart through most of the day, for more than a month.
6. You avoid meeting up with your friends for coffee or dinner for the fear of being judged or humiliating yourself in public. The last time you met them was over 2 months back.
7. There is consistent negative ongoing chatter in your mind as a result of which you experience lack of confidence in yourself and your abilities.

8. You save on pennies and worry excessively about any and every expense as more colleagues lose jobs. You are starting to compromise on your eating healthy foods, exercising and spending on essential medication.
9. You become acrimonious and distrustful to people around you as you feel you are being taken advantage of by those who surround you. This affects your relationship with those you loved and cared for.
10. You feel out of control through most of the day and overwhelmed with life in general. You end up feeling guilt-ridden over things you could not achieve in the day.

Indicators that point to seeking professional help

Through various studies, it has been observed that by and large if a person, in the medium term is not able to:

- Place a balanced perspective on things in life for the medium term.
- Give a meaning to their life or find a purpose for their living (i.e. find their significance in their world or scheme of things).
- Take life as it comes on most occasions and enjoy more than half of them.
- Cultivate and maintain a sense of humour and compassion.
- Reinvent and re-position themselves to adapt to the changing environment around them.
- Solve a majority of their problems by themselves or via consultation and support of their community.
- Maintain some focus and mental toughness despite trying times.

Then s/he requires professional help from a certified or licensed doctor to restore mental and emotional equilibrium.

This brings me to the third question of why is it then important to follow the practices chalked out in self-help books instead of seeing a psychologist to psychiatrist to begin with. There are three sides to that issue.

- First, a majority of the people who exhibit any of the aforesaid states even in the mid-term (period of 3 to 9 months), are able to allay those anxieties, fears and stress and some even overcome them through the practices books chalk out.
- Second, it is not advisable to prefer biological interference of medication at the first instance. After all, they are chemicals and any chemical potent enough to change the balance of chemicals inside your body, will be potent enough to have side effects – some of which are not desirable. The medications can be very effective, but they should not be thought of as a cure. Anxiety medication can provide temporary relief at best.
- Third, you will be weaned and eventually taken off medications by your prescribing doctor when they see improvement in chemical balance and behaviour. With the habit of the right practices and techniques inculcated through what books advise, you will be able to 'maintain' your healthy state easily. These lifestyle changes will act as support or complimentary activity so that you will not require returning to the doctor for help. Notice that the schedules and timetables that I have put forth through this book encourage the implementation of regular exercise, positive thinking, healthy eating, adequate sleep, minimal use of alcohol, nicotine, caffeine etc. All these help the various options that are available to you to treat your condition.

10 Things you need to know before you fix that appointment

At times when you are looking for quick fixes, you may be tempted to take the drug route. However, you must understand at all times that drugs will be prescribed up to a maximum of five years, beyond which time you are to have gained systemic/chemical equilibrium. You will eventually be weaned off them and expected to carry on the business of living without their help. Barring psychiatric drugs prescribed for acute conditions such as suicidal tendencies, PTSD, Parkinson's disease, dementia, manic episodes, schizophrenia and other similar illnesses, the treatment with drugs has a time course which after being run is expected to conclude.

Secondly, it is important to keep in mind that drugs will take time to reflect any improvement in your mental condition. Most drugs take anywhere between four to six weeks to have optimum influence in your system. It takes a certain amount of chemicals regulated at certain intervals for the desired level of the chemical to be reached in the blood to exhibit its allaying properties. So, just as it is not advised that you start on even over-the-counter drugs without the doctor's consultation, you should not stop the medication without their consultation because you do not see the results fast enough.

Thirdly, all medications will carry some undesirable side-effects. It is for you to check with your doctor's which side-effects he expects from the medicines he is prescribing for you. It is possible that you already have an underlying condition such as high cholesterol, or, are diabetic, in which case, you should not be taking or be prescribed certain drugs. In other words, you should come clean of your conditions to your doctor in case s/he does not run tests on you first to find out and depends on you to tell them.

Fourthly, though a single drug can exhibit five or more side-effects, every individual taking this drug will not experience all the five and no two individuals will show the same level of adverse effect. By the same corollary, two persons having the same condition may not be benefitted to the same extent by a drug prescribed to both of them.

Fifthly, drugs may aggravate the very symptoms it is addressing to treat in the short run as the body gets used to the introduction of a new and potent chemical in your body. So, it is very possible that a drug prescribed to treat anxiety will aggravate symptoms of anxiety such as palpitations, nervousness, dry throat, sweaty palms in the very short run before the body adapts to it and the optimum level of the drug enters your blood to be effective.

Sixthly, while you are on medication you will need to minimize the use of alcohol if not avoid it totally. Any substance that has the potential to spike neuron response will have impact on emotions, reactions and efficacy of the medication. It is for this reason that other substances such as nicotine, tobacco, caffeine usage should also be kept to bare minimum. If you are unable to reduce their intake, you need to bring it to light in your therapy session with your doctor.

Seventhly, we need to remember that just because therapy requires investments in time and money, it is not avoidable. You must continue with therapy until your doctor asks you to stop it. You may ask them first if you think it's time. Never stop therapy on your own. Therapies have graded process layouts that require you to familiarize at the sessions and put to practice at home and integrate into your lives. Your learning at the therapy sessions will form the basis of fire-fighting when the medications are stopped.

Eighthly, continue habit building. Just as with therapy, habits, activities charted out in this book will form your base in life whenever you come across stressful or adverse situations. They ensure that you do not experience negative outcomes and are able to handle the emotions in the appropriate way.

Ninthly, monitor your body's vitals and your progress. Psychiatric drugs often alter your body's cholesterol and blood sugar levels apart from kidney and liver functioning. Make sure you are getting these vitals tested at regular intervals such as, once every six months or as the doctor advises. Also chart your own progress by writing in your diary. Record your thoughts, emotions, challenges so that you can work them through with your doctor.

Not the least, you should be aware of the common side-effects that most drugs will exhibit in their course of administration. Here is a brief list of the most common afflictions:

- Disorientation and confusion
- Weight gain
- Nausea
- Loss of appetite
- Dizziness
- Drowsiness
- Speech difficulty
- Memory loss
- Hostility
- Depression
- Anxiety
- Hallucination and Sweating
- Palpitations
- Aggressive and Impulsive behaviour

Options in medication

Most psychiatric drug brands can be broadly classified into four major groups. There will of course be drugs within each group that will vary from another in the outcomes they deliver, side-effects, potency, duration of effect, part of the brain-body it affects, etc. However, these differences will vary and may even differ slightly between different brands that sport the same chemical. I have put together a basic list of drug groups, brands and ailments they cure and side effects they entail for you to take a look at.

Selective Serotonin Reuptake Inhibitor (SSRI):

DRUG GROUP	CHEMICAL	BRAND-NAME	TREATS	SIDE-EFFECTS
SSRI ANTI-DEPRESSANT	Citalopram	Celexa, Cipramil, Cipram, Dalsan, Recital, Emocal, Sepram, Seropram, Citox	Depression, anxiety disorders, personality disorders, phobias, insomnia, OCD	Nausea, anxiety, loss of libido, photo-sensitivity, apathy, weight gain, headache, fatigue, insomnia, rise in cholesterol and blood sugar levels, bruxism, urinary retention
	Escitalopram	Lexapro, Cipralex, Esertia		
	Fluoxetine	Prozac, Fontex, Seromex, Seronil, Sarafem, Ladose, Fluctin, Fluox, Depress, Lovan		
	Fluvoxamine	Luvox, Fevarin, Faverin, Dumyrox, Favoxil, Movox		
	Paroxetine	Paxil, Seroxat, Sereupin, Aropax, Deroxat, Divarius, Rexetin, Xetanor, Paroxat, Loxamine		
	Sertraline	Zoloft, Lustral, Serlain		

Tri-Cyclic Anti-Depressants (TCA):

This is another popular drug group that is used for similar symptoms and treatment of depression and related conditions, called the Tricyclic Anti-Depressants. However, SSRIs are now a preferred drug-group by most psychiatrists as they entail less severe side-effects than Tri-cyclic Antidepressants.

DRUG GROUP	CHEMICAL	BRAND-NAME	TREATS	SIDE-EFFECTS
TRI-CYCLIC ANTI-DEPRES-SANTS	Amitriptylinoxide	Amioxid, Ambivalon, Equilibrin	Depression	Dry mouth and nose, Blurred vision, constipation, urinary retention, cognitive and/or memory impairment, and increased body temperature, drowsiness, anxiety, apathy, changes in appetite and weight, sweating, sexual dysfunction, muscle twitches, weakness, nausea.
	Demexiptiline	Deparon, Tinoran		
	Desipramine	Norpramin, Pertofrane		
	Dibenzepin	Noveril, Victoril		
	Imipramine	Tofranil, Janimine, Praminil		
	Imipraminoxide	Imiprex, Elepsin		
	Melitracen	Deanxit, Dixeran, Melixeran, Trausabun		
	Propizepine	Depressin, Vagran		
	Protriptyline	Vivactil		

Other types of anti-depressants are Monoamine Oxidase (MAOs) and Norepinephrine Reuptake Inhibitors (NRIs). They work well on such persons on whom safer drugs do not produce the desired or expected results.

Monamine Oxidase

Chemical	Brand name
Phenelzine	Nardil
Isocarboxazid	Marplan
Tranylcypromine	Parnate

Monamine Oxidase

Chemical	Brand name
Bupropion	Amfebutamone, Wellbutrin,
Reboxetine	Edronax

Anxiolytics are anti-anxiety drug classification that includes Tranquilizers (both major and minor) and Benzodiazepines.

Minor Tranquilizers:

They treat debilitating anxiety and anxiety related disorders. They include drugs such as barbiturates, hydroxyzines and azapirones. These groups have the danger of being abused as they carry a high dependence factor.

AZAPIRONES

Chemical	Brand name
Buspirone	Buspar
Tandospirone	Sedeil
Gepirone	Ariza

Benzodiazepines:

They are used to treat withdrawal symptoms after long-term substance abuse, insomnia, anxiety, muscle spasm and as premedication in dental procedures, etc. They are essentially sedatives, muscle relaxants and amnesic in action. They also are anti-convulsants.

Chemical	Brand name
Lorazepam	Ativan
Clonazepam	Klonopin
Diazepam	Valium
Alprazolam	Xanax

Side effects include dizziness and drowsiness. It also includes feelings of euphoria, blurred vision, nausea, changes in appetite, aggressive behaviour, irritability and instances of impulsiveness apart from reported observations of visio-motor coordination, information processing, verbal learning and concentration.

Stimulants:

These psychoactive drugs[13] are anti-thesis of 'downers'. They have a stimulating or uplifting effect on the person using them. This means the person may experience increased physical and mental activity such as enhanced movement, alertness, wakefulness, arousal, motivation, endurance, heart rate, etc.

Common stimulants are nicotine, caffeine, cocaine, amphetamines (increasing norepinephrine and dopamine levels in our brain), norepinephrine reuptake inhibitors, norepinephrine-dopamine reuptake inhibitors and Modafinil, etc. Entertainment drugs such as Ecstasy (chemical name: Methylenedioxymethamphetamine) are often abused.

Drug sensitization, dependence, tolerance and withdrawal symptoms quickly arise with stimulants.

Mood Stabilizers:

They are those psychiatric drugs that suppress peaks in moods that fall between the extremes of mania and depression. All cases where the mood shift is severe, sustained and sudden are treated using mood stabilizers. Often a large number of anti-convulsants and anti-psychotics and other chemicals

---
15. Drugs that work on the central nervous system and alter the functioning of the brain.

are used as mood stabilisers. They especially suit patients of bipolar disorder, ADHD, dementia, delirium, mental retardation, intermittent explosive disorder, etc.

Side effects of mood stabilisers range from dizziness, headaches, nausea and bruising to hair loss, tremor, weight gain and sedation. There are many more side effects pertaining to each of the chemical groups mentioned in the list which you may check with your doctor if he/she has prescribed them. However, the side-effects mentioned in this note are common to all the anti-convulsants.

Anti-Convulsants

Chemical	Brand name
Carbamazepine	Tegretol
Divalproex Sodium	Depakote
Gabapentine	Neurontin
Lamotrigine	Lamictal
Oxcarbazepine	Trileptal
Topimarate	Topamax
Valproic Acid	Depakene

Anti-psychotic drugs or Major Tranquilizers:

Anti-psychotic drugs are prescribed chiefly to rein-in conditions of hallucinations, delusions and other psychosis. Patients of bipolar disorder and schizophrenics also find relief from them.

All anti-psychotic drugs have the drawback of long-term side-effects and so are not very popular unless the severity of the condition compels the doctor to prescribe them.

Some common side-effects are tremors, restlessness, sleepiness, nausea, increased saliva, muscle stiffness, abdominal pain, and urinary incontinence, abnormal vision.

Anti-psychotics

Chemical	Brand name
Resperidone	Risperdal
Olanzapine	Zyprexa
Clozapine	Clozaril
Quietiapine	Seroquel
Ziprasidone	Geodon
Asenapine	Saphris
Sertindole	Serdolect
Zotepine	Nipolept, Lodopin, Setous
Haloperidol	Haldol, Serenace
Chlorpromazine	Thorazine, Largactil
Fluphenazine	Prolixin
Perphenazine	Trilafon
Triflupromazine	Vesprin
Clopenthixol	Sordinol
Chlorprothixene	Cloxan, Taractan, Truxal

In conclusion

It is thus evident that psychiatric medications bring about more malaise and disturbing conditions in the medium and long term than they set out to suppress.

I am not propagating the non-usage of any drug; however it will be prudent to take all accounts into considerations before you decide on them. I wish to bring to light that though they should not be your preferred or first option at the signs of mental distress, they will have to be resorted to in certain cases of acuity. In the ultimate analysis for considering the route to psychiatric drugs to help you tide over your mental discomfort/condition, you need to ask yourself some very important and relevant questions. A short sample list could look like this:

1) Is medication the only option for my problem?
2) What non-drug treatments could help me?
3) What self-help strategies might help me get my condition under control?
4) What expenses and investments of time am I looking at for non-drug treatments such as cognitive-behavioural therapy?
5) Am I willing and can I afford to chance with undesirable side effects of medication?
6) Will the medication have effect on my pre-existing medical condition such as blood pressure, etc., and the medications I take for them?
7) How long will I need to be on those prescription drugs?
8) Will taking the drugs hamper my lifestyle – work, home and other activities, diets, socializing, etc.?
9) Will the drugs cause dependency issues making withdrawal difficult?
10) What is the prognosis for my condition?

Once you have the answers to these questions and you and your family are involved in collective decision making, you may choose to opt for taking the route of drugs. But the process of information collection and careful considerations of the answers will help you and your family make informed decisions.

Daily dozen - activities that keep your brain ticking

I have put together a rudimentary list of activities you can do to keep yourself mentally fit, alert and ticking. Yes, they will go a long way in staving off senior moments and the natural neural degeneration that occurs with ageing. You may add your own ideas for activities that you can combine with some I have chalked out below that you find interesting.

A list of activities to keep your brain young

1. Change the order of performing everyday activities
2. Count numbers backwards, say your alphabets in reverse order
3. Crosswords, Sudoku, Puzzles
4. Exercise, dance with changed routine and steps
5. Learn a new language, software, recipe
6. Learn focusing techniques
7. Meditate
8. Practice deep and controlled breathing
9. Read half a page of a book and check if you can recall
10. Take different road routes to places
11. Use the non-dominant hand to do some chores
12. Visualise, set goals, measure, correct with everyday chores

EMOTIONAL FITNESS

"The walls we build around us to keep sadness out also keeps out the joy."

Jim Rohn (1930-2009)
Entrepreneur, author and motivational speaker

Through the Barricades to Meet Yourself

Evolution from emotional fitness to emotional wellness

Emotional fitness does the spade work to elevate you to a state of emotional wellness. This implies that emotional fitness is a component to attaining the end of emotional wellness, and there are the other cogs in the wheel that work as a team. The other nuts and bolts are physical and mental fitness. My book, The Urban Woman's Integrated Fitness Guide already speaks on the rationale and practices to reach the goal of physical fitness and section one of this book gives pointers on how to keep yourself mentally agile.

So how does one achieve the seemingly all-elusive end of emotional wellness? To start with, emotional wellness is arrived at by putting small slices of everyday time into practicing physical, mental and emotional fitness techniques. Emotional wellness will offer peace, well-balanced emotions (as opposed to a frustrating lack of emotions or an overwhelming flurry of emotions), and a happy and correct perspective of life's offerings, and, of course, contentment with and in the present personal surroundings and situations.

At this point, you may wonder what exactly the role of emotional fitness is. To put it simply, it entails mood regulation, handling of common everyday situations that involve different degrees of stress with the right emotional responses, training yourself to feel good, bringing about work-life balance, gaining better control of life's choices, gaining emotional strength, knowledge of your old response patterns. Of course, to be able to do all of these meaningfully, you need to start at a place where you know are at present so that paving the way forward is easy.

Emotional, physical and mental fitness – the awesome threesome!

We have seen in our own lives (as well as in the life of those of sports' greats playing in tournaments and championships; and entertainment celebrities on reality and talent shows), that when we lose the edge of our physical fitness then we also experience losing hold of our emotions. The vice-versa is also true. Try to remember the last time you were bored and lonely, you were unable to eat or play effectively during the period? Similarly, mental fitness is catenated to emotional fitness as well. The day you wake up feeling negative or get stressed with work or traffic, your emotions go astray too. Have you also observed that the day you feel depressed, you cannot focus or think clearly? Herein emerges the linkages of mental, physical and emotional fitness.

Switching the tone to positives, note that the day you work out well at the gym or at home or outdoors, you come back home feeling content with life and better able to deal with life's situations. You feel stronger and in more control of life's choices, so you are able and willing to focus more on a given job at hand. In other words, you are more mentally agile besides being emotionally balanced and physically fit at this point.

On the assumption that you are keeping at physical fitness (through daily workouts, eating right and preventing injuries, etc.) and mental fitness (through practice of positive thinking, mental activities, relaxation through meditation and focus workouts, etc.), let us look at the elements to achieving emotional fitness. But before we are able to do that, we need a quick realty check on where we stand today. Here is a brief exercise along with it's rationale that will help us do just that.

The 15-minute self-evaluation of emotions

Rationale of the Inspection to Introspection Questionnaire:

I have termed the self-survey list as 'The Inspection to Introspection Questionnaire', because as you proceed into the questionnaire you will notice that the questions demand you to introspect rather than provide information at first instance. This self-awareness is the first step towards trend-breaking and makes all the difference in establishing desirable habits that will fetch us desirable results. Through this technique it aims to size up the basic aspects of your emotional stability, your response and reaction to people, circumstances and places. To be able to do this questionnaire honestly, you will need more than a couple of seconds to come close to the truth. The truer you are to yourself and in your responses the more precise your results will be about you.

- My advice to you before you begin on the assessment is that you pick your choice of the answer for all the questions first and then go back to mark them with the score table provided on the next page. This way you will avoid the temptation to look into the scores of the following question and re-adjust your response.

The Inspection to Introspection Questionnaire

Moving from Inspection to Introspection in 15 minutes

1. How often do you feel depressed or sad?
    a. Rarely. Say, once every couple of months. I am not very sensitive.
    b. Not often. Once a month, maybe.
    c. Often – Once a week.
2. How do you tackle your depression?

    a. I distract myself with hobbies, friends.
    b. I try to sleep it away and think about it in the waking hours.
    c. I cry, feel blue and helpless.
3. Are your appetite and weight healthy?
    a. Yes. I think I am ok but have not checked.
    b. I overeat when I crave for foods and I may be overweight.
    c. I do not eat enough and am underweight.
4. Do you feel happy with your overall look?
    a. I think I am reasonably presentable.
    b. I wish I was slimmer so that I could feel attractive.
    c. I wish I was thinner/plumper, to feel more loved.
5. How do you deal with conflicts with friends or at work?
    a. I do not specifically work on the conflict after it has happened. I think things and people will come around given the time.
    b. I work it out with the colleague, I talk and apologize if need be.
    c. I worry about it because it makes me prone to losing my appetite, sleep and makes me anxious.
6. Would you prefer the company of friends or would rather be alone?
    a. I am ok with both.
    b. I love to be with friends and around people all the time.
    c. I like to spend time with myself. I am uncomfortable with people around.
7. Do you have close friends you can confide in, talk to or depend in times of need?
    a. I have a large circle but no such close friends. I can discuss what I need to with them.
    b. A couple of them.
    c. Not really.

8. If you are upset, disappointed or angry with someone, how do you express it usually?
   a. At that time, I may raise my voice and swear vengeance, but when things resolve, I generally don't carry the emotion far.
   b. I feel outraged and often think of hitting or hurting the person.
   c. I feel taken advantage of and want to scream or cry.
9. You move into a new neighbourhood or join a new office
   a. You watch the people around before you familiarize with them.
   b. You take no time to get comfortable in your new surroundings.
   c. You take your own time to get to know the people and places around.
10. When was the last time you did something to improve yourself – diet, exercise, learn a new language or technology?
    a. A couple of months back.
    b. Why, I am on it right now.
    c. I work now and do not have the time for such things.
11. You are sitting at home in the living room watching TV with your parents when your child or pet or best friend enters the room and heads straight for a hug. Do you
    a. Hug the person back and continue to another room to converse.
    b. Hug and peck, pretending to feel as if nothing has happened and continue to watch TV.
    c. Squirm with shyness at open display of emotions that you suspect is expected out of you, such as a kiss, a hug, etc.
12. Which would describe your feelings more now –
    a. Resentment of the past, happiness with the present, worry about the future.

b. Happiness of the past, sorrow in the present, hope for the future.
c. Resentment of the past, sorry for the present and anxious of the future.

SCORE

1.	a. 3	b. 2	c. 1
2.	a. 3	b. 2	c. 1
3.	a. 3	b. 2	c. 1
4.	a. 3	b. 1	c. 1
5.	a. 2	b. 3	c. 1
6.	a. 2	b. 3	c. 1
7.	a. 2	b. 3	c. 1
8.	a. 3	b. 1	c. 2
9.	a. 2	b. 3	c. 1
10.	a. 2	b. 3	c. 1
11.	a. 3	b. 2	c. 1
12.	a. 2	b. 2	c. 1

12 – 19 You seem to be apprehensive of the people around you and of the situations you are faced with. Because you feel taken advantage of, you keep to yourself, have low self-esteem and do not trust easily. In a vicious cycle, you are in little control of your emotions and give in to the 'victim' role of crying or demonstrating helplessness which again could be misutilised by those around you, further reinforcing your beliefs.

20 -27 You represent most of us. You seem to experience bouts of loss of emotional control and a fair degree of lack of self-esteem. Though you are largely balanced, it would be good to spend a little more time with yourself and see where you need to tweak yourself – appearances or emotional flexibility. Your trump card is your network of support in your family, friends and colleagues and this itself largely provides your stability to you.

26 – 37 Your emotional stability is drawn chiefly of being unaware and/or unbothered about the life's small stuff. Though you could spruce up on healthy living and self-improvement by being aware of the need to evolve at a personal level more, you are largely happy as you are. You could consider the spiritual recommendations in this book to give yourself a new leaf to explore!

This questionnaire, just as any other, will only give you a ballpark indication of what you should be looking at in this book. On the assumption that most of us score anywhere between 16 and 25, the following pages will contain common areas of emotional upheaval and how best you can manage them.

Erasing the Emotional Scars – Tackling the sticky six

Scores are exactly what they are – pointers or indicators that tell you where you are roughly at and which direction you should be headed. They are by no means a statement of your personality or your capabilities. They should be taken in that perspective only. Remember, we all change and are constantly on the path to evolution or devolution. Even while you are reading this sentence, millions of cells have undergone changes in your digestive, endocrine and nervous systems. As with all life and non-life, changes are the defining and permanent feature of the universe. So the scores, at best are a rough and ready photo shot of a moment in time that only hint at where lacunae exist at this instance and where improvements can be done.

A first level score (Scores between 12-19) may look undesirable but it could also mean you are sensitive about other people's feelings and care about those around you. It may also reflect that you do not expect them to harm you in any way and expect a return of trust – all of which exhibit the good in you.

Similarly a second level score (those between 20-27) may look optimal but may mean you are more than desirably externally dependent for your own stability, which may not necessarily be a good thing. On the other hand, it may point that your occasional loss of emotional control allows people around you to be a little careful of you–thus not taking you for granted!

Lastly the most evolved score slab (that between 28-36) may mean that you are a little insensitive to those around you. It may also reflect that you have not spent enough time with yourself towards spiritual development and are often unaware of the reactions of those you interact with and of the playing out of events around you. You need to be more alive!

As you just saw, all good could be only superficially so and all bad can actually embed some pleasing attributes. Scores that you score in the tests given in the book or given anywhere else should not define you for any long period of time. It is in this regard more than any other that we must consistently be aware of the change patterns and flux in us and those people, things and circumstances around us.

Unfortunately, most of us forget this very often and our own temporary but flawed perspective of ourselves begins to take root through repetitive behavioural patterns that we find hard to let go off and reinforcements and sometimes even approval of the behaviour or reaction from those around us. This is when we find ourselves going downhill on the path of emotional stability.

Though no book can possibly cover the myriad situations in which we can sway away from our emotional equilibrium, I have put together six common circumstances that occur at some point in most of our lives and rock our cradle. I have also given techniques of how to manage or tackle such situations when you find yourself in the grips of emotional rollercoaster for longer than you should be. I use the terms 'should be' because, some emotional venting is necessary to remain emotionally and mentally healthy and physically active. However, when the grips of emotions start to damage the walls of these very components of mental and physical health, you know you have treaded the path long enough and it is time to resurrect. Your first approach should be to bring about healing on your own and in your own terms. It is desirable at this point to involve anyone who is close to you that you can trust. Most of us respond positively to damage-control techniques at this stage itself provided the diagnosis and action are quick. However, if you are those few who have more faith in seeking professional help, you should not shy away from it.

1. Abridging anger

Exhibited anger is an expression of aggressive behaviour or aggression. Though expressing anger is at times both necessary and healthy, it is the frequent displays of anger - exhibited or implied; frequent/regular, uncontrolled, overt and impulsive that is unhealthy and undesirable. It's common to observe that men are more openly demonstrative about their anger often backing it with raised voice, hand-action etc. than women. With the coming of the progressive age, women are more comfortable expressing their anger in similar ways, though a majority of this populace still expresses anger in indirect and non-physical ways.

It is important to learn ways to cut short your anger. Even before you can demonstrate your anger to achieve a premeditated goal, you will host a good number of emotions and symptoms that are first harmful to you. Feelings of irritation, rage, tachycardia, rise in blood pressure and body temperature, hot flashes, rapid breathing and pulse will damage your inner systems with a surge of adrenaline etc. before you can inflict any verbal harm on your target to attain the desired effect.

I have worked out a basic questionnaire which can help you ascertain where in the scale of anger coefficient you stand and if you require self or professional help to even out the abberated behaviour. The questionnaire is based on a True or False rationale and scores are assigned to the numbers of each you gain. The underlying principle to scoring and their meaning are given at the end of the test.

Erasing the Emotional Scars – Tackling the sticky six

Think before you answer your question so that a more accurate picture emerges. There are questions that crosscheck your honesty in the questionnaire, so stay close to reality while answering them. Self-help techniques are drawn out in detail thereafter to help you overcome the menace of anger.

Analyzing Anger – 15 Questions That will Help Reflect and Consolidate

Q. No	Question	Option	
1.	I get very disturbed and angry when I think of the people who have done me wrong in the past.	T	F
2.	I feel that I have been betrayed often by people I have trusted in the past.	T	F
3.	When I feel betrayed or angry, I want to get even with them.	T	F
4.	I find it hard to forgive or forget.	T	F
5.	Some of my colleagues, friends and family are afraid of my anger spills.	T	F
6.	I have had bad arguments with those who I love the most.	T	F
7.	During an anger outburst I feel like or have broken things or hit people.	T	F
8.	After an outburst of anger, I feel sick and avoid meeting the receiver of my anger.	T	F
9.	The thought of killing the wrong-doer or committing suicide has occurred to me many times in fits of anger.	T	F
10.	When angry I say things that I often regret later.	T	F
11.	I feel justified in telling what I have told when angry.	T	F

Q. No	Question	Option
12.	I obsess about arguments, fights after they are over.	T F
13.	After an argument, outburst or fight, I later feel I could have handled the situation better, replied better, etc.	T F
14.	I resort to drugs, alcohol, etc. to cope with anger episodes	T F
15.	My job and/or relationships are in danger because of my temper.	T F

Scoreboard

Score Range	Comment
>= 6 True	You are nearing danger levels and your job; relations are in danger of damage. Change is the need of the hour. You may begin with self-help tools given in this book. If you see no improvement, you may want to seek professional help.
4-6 True	Most of us fall into this score range. You can use the self-help techniques given in this book to improve upon your anger reactions.
True - Qs 7, 9 and 14	You must seek medical and professional help as soon as possible.

Mentor Your Mind

Fortunately for us, there are many ways in which we can address our anger problem. The pointers below will give you an outline of what you can do at your end that will see you through your predicament. Unless, you have reasons to consult a medical professional immediately (such as anger reactions bordering on hitting, killing or suicide), it is advisable that you try these highly effective methods before you decide on professional assistance.

Erasing the Emotional Scars – Tackling the sticky six 89

Anger Help Counter

1. **Changing Your Lifestyle Patterns**
   a. It is possible that your life is packed with too many chores and must-dos making you stressed and leaving you feeling overwhelmed. Under such a situation, it is normal to feel irritable and possibly misdirect your frustrations on those around you. If you are snapping, disagreeing and arguing often with family and colleagues, it is clear you are operating under daily pressure. This could be unhealthy at other levels

- Changing Your Lifestyle Patterns
- Emotion Control
- Cognitive Behavioral Therapy
- Support Groups
- Professional Help
- Coping with Confrontation
- Regular Self-evaluation
- Assertiveness Training
- Knowing When to Disconnect

besides straining relationships with co-workers and family members. It could harm your health giving you hypertension, dizziness, etc.

You need to step back and take a look at a typical work day or if you want to establish a more meaningful trend and solution, take a whole week as an observation unit and analyse it. Are there tasks you can prioritize? Tasks such as immediate and daily deliverables, weekly deliveries can be scheduled so that you are at peace as to when to do them. This will also help you from missing important things.

b. Are you over-committing yourself and your time? A lot of us, me included are over-ambitious with our time and work. This is not to doubt your ability to have them done but it does wind us up, racing against time, leaving no margin for rest which is unhealthy. Spend 5-7 minutes before the start of each day to draw out your program for the day. While chalking out your day be reasonable with time and workload.

c. Learn to say 'No'. People who take more on to their plate are also the ones assigned more tasks at office. This comes from a mix of both 'taken for granted' attitude towards your capabilities, habit to complete the job and your time as well as an element of 'let's set this person up' sadism on the part of others. Recognize the patterns and learn to say 'No' when you need to and when you think you are either being set up for failure or can't cope. An occasional 'No' will not let them take you for granted but also will help you consistently re-evaluate your own work list and prioritize them.

d. Set aside half-hour for yourself. Yes, trite as it sounds, this is an essential to-do! This half hour could be dedicated to either an activity you enjoy doing such as listening to music, watching sitcoms, window-shopping or dedicated to self-improvement such as learning a new skill, or learning ways to manage your anger better! This time will help you disconnect temporarily to the rest of the day and will work as a rejuvenator.

2. **Emotion Control**
   a. This involves the learning of breathing techniques that will help you relax and stay calm even in the face of anger. What it does is to enable you to get angry only at the mental level and keeps you safe emotionally and physically from the ill-effects of anger. You may follow this particular breathing technique even while seated upright in your office chair. However, it is preferable to do it sitting on the floor or in lying down position.
      i. Sit with a straight back.
      ii. Take a deep breath, completely filling your lungs.
      iii. Hold on to the breath to a slow count of three.
      iv. Slowly exhale to a count of six.
      v. Repeat steps ii to iv, 6-10 times.
   b. Emotions may also be put a rein on by distracting yourself productively. Suppose you feel like yelling at your co-worker or child for doing something you had made clear repeatedly not to do, you may distract yourself temporarily to wade over this unwanted reaction by taking time off in the rest rooms or looking at another task at the list and attend to it before addressing your colleague or child with a calmer disposition.

3. **Cognitive Behavioural Therapy (CBT)**

CBT helps us improve our state of mind, confidence and self-image thereby enabling us to tackle any emotional state in a more effective way. It uses analytical and self-observation tools to drive home a point. CBT will rectify the way we interpret our own experiences as well as the way in which we express and control anger.

A typical CBT program to manage anger will involve:
a. Approaches to relaxation and stress management,
b. Identification of negative thought patterns,
c. Testing them as hypothesis,
d. Identifying the errors in logic of the sufferer and then substituting them for a balanced approach,
e. It will also provide support therapy to prevent relapse of destructive behavioural patterns, and,
f. Work on our issues with mistrust, subjugation, vulnerability, etc.

4. Support Groups

There will be the local support groups with people who experience similar difficulties with anger. It is recommended that you meet them. This will reduce your sense of isolation meeting other people to realise you are not alone in your dilemma. Talking to these people will help you lessen your emotional and mental burden, will give you a group that understands you completely and will also help you learn techniques they will be sharing and those that have worked for them from time to time. It is a win-win association. Find out where the local chapter of anger group is and sign up.

5. Professional Help

Professional help is important when:
a. Your anger is turning violent and you consider or have hit someone.
b. When you contemplate murder or suicide.
c. When anger management is a chronic condition with you.
d. You are not deriving any benefit from self-help techniques.

Clinical psychologists, psychiatrist, behavioural scientists can all help you with your problem. Be prepared to take medication if your doctor so prescribes. They know what is best for you at the given moment. You may however ask about its duration, dosage, potency, side-effects while you are in consultation.

There will also be anger management programs being run by health professionals in your city or town of which you can find about and join. They will give you effective tools and techniques to calm your anger emotions through their day-courses that run over a few weeks.

6. Coping With Confrontation

When you find yourself in the middle of a confrontation at work or at home or elsewhere and feel as though you are losing control of your emotions, you will do good to remember that:

a. The other person needs to be heard before we speak and that it is alright for them to hold a different point of view on a matter.

b. While you are giving an ear to the person you may utilise the time to breathe in the way mentioned earlier, so that you remain calm.

c. You can also use the time to chalk out what you need to say to this person. This is a critical task.

d. It is possible that the person did not understand you the first time and you would require undoing the person's misunderstanding before you address your view.

e. While you do this, stick to the topic at hand, there is no reason to get personal on work environments or elsewhere.

7. Regular Self-Evaluation

While you are helping yourself by listing out situations that set you off on an anger trail or other negative thought and action patterns, and learning skills to deflect anger away from your life and building constructive dialogue with your inner self, you must remember to evaluate yourself at regular intervals to see if you are reaching short term and medium term goals, if you need to improvise and readjust to get back on track. Just as we need to explore our past experiences to analyse the base of our current anger patterns, choosing happy emotions, developing empathetic understanding of other's problems, forgiveness, assumptions of basic good nature of the person etc., we also need to see where we stand regarding each of these issues. A short and ready-made evaluation list can be made so that it is at hand for assessment. You may have many copies of it to do this activity over every week or 10 days. Keep the previous week's evaluation sheet to gauge your progress or stability.

Observation	Response	
I have had an anger outburst this week.	Yes	No
I am following several self-help techniques.	Yes	No
I am considering CBT or anger management programs.	Yes	No
I came up with one Win-Win solution to a situation this week.	Yes	No
Time out or forgiveness are some things I have to work on.	Yes	No

8. Assertiveness Training

Consistently remind yourself to make win-win choices. Be specifically aware of this, when you are expecting instigation from some quarter that will set you on fire. You can start by:

   a. Making a list of all self-destructive emotions like swearing, yelling, throwing etc., and replace them with constructive emotions like discussions, talking, breathing, etc.
   b. You can also include activities such as painting, reading, calming music, workouts, sleeping that will calm you as a person.
   c. Learn ways to be constructive in your problem-solving and confrontation situation rather than impulsive and destructive.

9. Knowing When and How to Disconnect

Disconnecting or learning to switch off can be learnt at anger management programs or at your therapist. It can also be learnt by taking a 'time out' or choosing to come back to the problem after a short while. You do not have to attend to it then and there or come up with a reply, retort or response/solution. You can tell that you can't think straight now or are busy with a client at hand and will get back to it in half an hour. This gives you the time to feel the anger, calm down and assess the situation more logically rather than come with off the cuff responses. You may implement this as often as you need to and anywhere in life.

2. Boredom and loneliness

Living urban and busy lives often leaves us little time for friends. By the time you return from office on weekdays, it's time to fix a quick dinner, eat, run emergency groceries and watch a little television that serves as downtime before heading for bed. Some of us are even able to fit in a dash of workouts to keep our health and conscience in the right place. Quite often some of us have to bring back some office work home to be able to deliver them the next day. If you have a family or parents that stay with you, you are even more tight for personal time. Weekends are often spent catching up with pending personal work such as laundry, bank work etc. visiting friends or joining recreational classes or groups of like-minded people. It is no wonder that quite a few of us feel that our life lacks zing and variety of choice. Over a period of time, boredom and loneliness sets into life and you lose interest in things that are going on around you.

Look at these thoughts and statements. Do they sound like you?

- I prefer to be alone.
- I am not as excited about activities I used to once enjoy.
- I am not very comfortable with the presence of people around me.
- I do not have close friends.

- I think people assume that you will enjoy doing all the things in groups and as per their choice.
- I cannot laugh at myself.

If you agree on even three of these statements, chances are that you are not very social and often get bored and experience loneliness.

Mentor Your Mind

Proceeding on the assumption that you either lack the volition or the time to indulge in mingling with friends, I have developed a little routine you could follow. This schedule basically gives you an idea on what is possible in that limited time available at your disposal or how you could still enjoy living being by yourself if you base yourself on hobby building – those that require only you to learn and do. As you start to roll with the schedule, you can modify some of the activities and hobbies by adding or substituting your own activities to bring variation and to sustain interest over a period of time as well as to suit work timings and seasons!

Type	Pre-Office	Post-Office
Weekdays	1. Outdoor yard work / gardening or indoor gardening 2. Reading 3. Learning a new language 4. Workout	1. Cooking – new recipes 2. Time with your pet cat, dog, bird, etc. 3. Crossword/ Sudoku 4. Meditation

It is evident that these activities will take up almost all of your time and weekend. If you are familiar with an activity, you can research more about it and try new things – such as learn more about different types of workouts, more on pet care or deeper on the subject of gardening. A lot of knowledge is available online from trusted resources for a payment. Note that bedtimes are not crammed with activities as it is time to slow down and relax rather than rejuvenate.

Erasing the Emotional Scars – Tackling the sticky six 97

If you are comfortable spending time with a friend or family, you may partner your activities with them or include some people in one activity and others in the remaining ones. A lot of variations can be brought about to suit your personal needs. Leading a life such as this, will make it more fun, meaningful and utilise your time more productively than sitting innumerable hours in front of the television set or at the internet, which are both unhealthy activities at long stretch. These activities as mentioned in the table will also go a long way to develop you as a well-rounded person and enable you to live a fuller, more enriched life.

Type	Morning	Afternoon	Evening	Before bedtime
Saturdays	1. Outdoor yard work / gardening or indoor gardening 2. Learning a new language 3. Workouts	1. Reading 2. Cooking new recipes 3. Walk in the park with pet or children 4. Painting 5. Get sunshine – step out	1. Hobby class – pottery, painting, etc 2. Writing 3. Office work	1. Crossword/ Sudoku etc. 2. Meditation 3. Television etc.
Sundays	1. Meditation 2. Learning new language 3. Workouts 4. Reading 5. Religious duties (church service, satsang, etc.) 6. Step out – get sunshine	1. Community Service 2. Grocery, Laundry 3. City Sightseeing 4. Gardening 5. Writing 6. Cafe visits	1. Tutoring 2. Cooking 3. Television 4. New skill development 5. Pet care 6. Shopping or window shopping	1. Reading 2. Self-care

3. Darkness after a death in the family

Whether we are mentally in-the-knowledge of a near one's approaching death (say due to being diagnosed with a fatal condition), we are never really ready at so many levels. And when the inevitable happens, we are in shock and it hurts just as badly as it would had it come upon us suddenly.

It is also true that those of us experiencing the loss undergo the oft-written about phases – denial, disbelief, anger, humiliation, bargaining, depression, guilt, sadness and acceptance. Yet each one of us is unique and take our own varying time at each one of these stages of grieving. It will not be right to say that spending more than 'x' number of weeks at a particular phase is a sign of damage starting to incur on our health, but it will be precise to say that being at any one stage for a period that starts to make us feel worthless, leads to illusions, thoughts of self-destruction, depression and causes inability to function normally is a sign of the alarm bells going off and it is time you be aware of your own needs and seek help.

To start with, it is acceptable among social and medical circles worldwide that the person experiencing grief will find it hard to eat or sleep, may dream or hear the dead person, be forgetful or indulge in any other activity excessively, experience some physical stress apart from the expected mental and emotional stress, become withdrawn and give in to frequent crying. No matter how helpless or fearful you feel, it is important that you go through these emotions. Stubbing feelings will lead to other underlying mental and physical conditions later. This has been proved scientifically. If you feel like letting go for a couple of days or a week or two, this is perfectly normal. You should neither panic, worry nor feel guilty for your behaviour for the supposed 'inconvenience' you think you are causing to those around you. This is your grief, your loss and trauma that you feel and is your way of coping and healing.

However, be aware that if your trauma is not letting you grieve, it is time you seek help from friends, family and the doctors. Trauma will specially be intensely felt if the death of the dear one is unexpected – such as a suicide or a murder, accident, etc. The trauma may be so severe that you may always feel on tenterhooks, fearful or even re-live the incident internally and avoid any conversation that hints at the episode. When this begins to happen, the preoccupation of these symptoms does not allow for grieving and becomes harmful for you.

When you are in the process of mourning and feeling the loss of the near one, be patient with yourself. It can take as much as 1-2 years to heal completely and even then you will have brief memories of the person a couple of times in the day. If you see yourself running into trouble, ask for your friend's or family's help. If they are not around, seek professional help.

Mentor Your Mind

1. Take care of your health

At all times take care of your health. Much as this sounds both obvious and banal, it is one we often forget. With friends and family moving in and out of the house often and the sadness of the loss affecting appetite and sleep, your physical health is the first thing that takes a beating. Some of us who are hit particularly hard by the incident may use substance, sleeping pills and other medications or alcohol excessively to 'cope' with their grief. Be wary that you do not step into such a situation. If you even suspect falling into such a trap, seek medical help from a professional. Rest as often as you can through all this as it is likely that you feel loss of energy and fatigued with worry, sorrow and anxiety.

2. Seek out a friend you can talk to

No one expects you to tide over such a loss all by yourself. Reaching out for a close friend or someone you are comfortable with in the family is not a sign of weakness. Some families and friends who were earlier distant actually come together at times of crises. Death is a great equalizer and afflicts each one of our lives, so the reality and enormity of death is alive with each one of us that helps people to step forward, put aside differences to pitch in times of need. Feel free to share your thoughts, fears, dilemmas, emotions with a close one. It is unhealthy to keep pent up feelings to yourself.

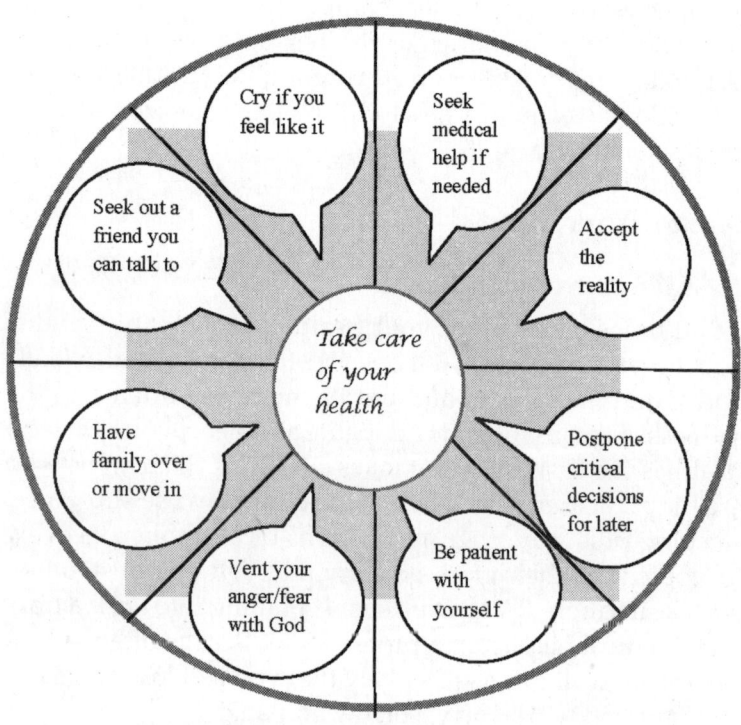

The Coping Wheel - 9 Things You Can Do To Lessen the Harshness of Death

Share your sadness and apprehensions. This enables you to come out of the grieving process faster.

3. Do not pent up your feelings – Cry!

It is perfectly normal to cry. You should neither be embarrassed nor be sorry for it. In fact it is important to cry and let go of the pent up emotions of sorrow, loss, despair etc. Kept inside, these emotions may later infest into mental and physical conditions with serious outcomes. In some cultures, a person who is too shocked to cry, is often slapped so that they begin the crying such that process of expunging emotions begins.

4. Seek medical help if needed

There is always a possibility that sharing your grief with friends or family does not help you through with your sorrow or it may be that you have no one close at hand. It may also be that though help is at hand, you see yourself taking undesirable medication or using alcohol to tide over your loss. You may be entertaining suicidal and other similar self-destructive thoughts. In case, you are not comfortable sharing every detail you need to share with a known person, you can always seek assistance by seeing a psychologist. They are trained at handling such situations and know what works or how to get you out of a dependence habit. Seeking professional help is a sign of your strength to accept your problem and awareness to put it right.

5. Accept reality

Just as death is a reality of life whether we arrive at it sooner or later, so is life. We have been blessed with life, to live it. We must inch slowly to pave the way forward. Though this may be easier said than done, you must consistently remind yourself that there are people around you such as a child or spouse who loves and needs you and may even be dependent on you. In due course of months, see if you can be in the present moment for minutes together.

6. Defer taking any critical decisions at this time

You will be emotional and are likely to be driven by sentimental feelings at this stage. It is possible that non-practical and possibly imprudent decisions be made by you on the basis of those thoughts – such as selling of property, writing out an unbalanced will or giving the power of attorney to dispense yourself of authority you have over assets, re-marrying, changing jobs or residence etc. Resist the temptation to do so, no matter how the circumstances are unfolding. There will be a time to take financial and legal decisions with more balance and a better perspective. If possible seek legal help.

7. Be patient with yourself

Do not expect the normal from yourself. Things will change and you will function (think and act) normally in due course of time. Be patient with yourself. It is very easy to feel frustrated at your lack of focus or depression. We are all humans. Robots operate at the switch of buttons. We are all made of emotions. Give yourself time to normalise. Stay away from those who give timelines on returning to 'normalcy'. Each one of us is unique and heals in their own time – some earlier, some later.

8. Vent your anger on God

Most people feel, cheated, wronged, humiliated towards the later stages of mourning the loss of a close one. This makes them lose faith in God and makes them challenge His presence. It makes them angry why they are being made to go through the situation. This is an expected phase and you must go through all the stages by yourself to be able to heal well. Venting on God is far healthier than opting for self-damaging acts.

9. Have family over or move in

You are experiencing a very personal and emotional upheaval. You are not expected to wing it alone. In fact, researches show that both grieving and recovery from loss is better gone through if in the company of loving people. This way you are less likely to take untoward decisions and act impulsively. If you do not feel comfortable moving in with a friend or family, request them to move in for a few days or weeks.

4. Dungeons of depression

The American Psychiatrists Association's current Diagnostic and Statistical Manual on Mental Disorders IV-TR[16] states that if you display primarily a depressed mood and a loss of interest in events or surroundings around you, you are likely to be in a depressed state. This especially is the case when the signs are prolonged into many days or weeks together.

DSM-IV-TR[16] goes on to add that if you display any of the four symptoms below, it can be medically termed as clinical depression.

1. Overwhelming sadness or fear or inability to feel emotions.
2. Loss of appetite or binge eating with corresponding change in body weight.
3. Reduced memory.
4. Thoughts of death or suicide.
5. Lack of focus.
6. Low self-esteem.
7. Consistent fatigue.

---

16. A text revision of *DSM-IV*, called *DSM-IV-TR*, was published in July 2000. The primary goal of *DSM-IV-TR* was to maintain the currency of the *DSM-IV* text, which reflected the empirical literature up to 1992. Thus, most of the major changes in *DSM-IV-TR* were confined to the descriptive text. Changes were made to a handful of criteria sets in order to correct errors identified in *DSM-IV*. In addition, some of the diagnostic codes were changed to reflect updates to the *International Classification of Diseases, Ninth Edition, Clinical Modification* (ICD-9-CM) coding system adopted by the U.S. government.

8. Disturbed sleep patterns – insomnia, etc.
9. Disinterest in pleasurable activities.
10. Living sedately.
11. Thoughts of inflicting self injury.
12. Feelings of anxiety, guilt or hopelessness, etc.

If you consider yourself alone in the fight against a basket of these merciless symptoms, you need to think again. The WHO in association with SEARO published a report[17] stating the following facts:

- Nearly 5-10% of persons in a community at a given time are in need of help for depression.
- As much as 8-20% of persons carry the risk of developing depression during their lifetime.
- The average age of the onset of major depression is between 20 and 40 years.
- Women have higher rates of depression than men.
- Race or ethnicity does not influence the prevalence of depression.

And went ahead to clearly define the risk groups as:

- Women are at greater risk than men.
- Separated and divorced people.
- A person having a close family member with depression.
- Early parental loss.
- Negative stressful events and chronic stress.

---

17. World Health Organization Regional Office South for East Asia. Report on Mental Health and Substance Abuse called 'Conquering Depression' was prepared by experts from the Region provides valuable information for the lay public and policy-makers regarding the current state of knowledge about depression. More importantly, it describes ways and means by which anyone "can get out of the blues".
URL: http://www.searo.who.int/en/Section1174/Section1199/Section1567/Section1826_8101.htm

- Lack of social support.
- Family type and those living in urban areas compared to rural areas.

One can only imagine the worldwide figures on depression if these are the numbers for the SEAR countries (Bangladesh, Bhutan, DPR Korea, India, Indonesia, Maldives, Myanmar, Nepal, Sri Lanka, Thailand, Timor-Leste).

Regardless of the global statistics and how many of the emotions you experience from the list given by institutions of psychiatric condition, they will be personal and harrowing to you. The feeling of hopelessness is very real and the willingness to do anything of value is abysmal. So is there anything you can really do to help yourself out of this condition? The answer is a resounding 'Yes!' and many have helped themselves out of depressive states unless medically proven chronic. After all, 25% of all of us in this world will experience depression at one time or another in our lives. Let's see how best we are able to cope with the evils of the condition and keep nuisance to the manageable minimum.

Mentor Your Mind

1. **Seek Family Or Medical Help**: If you look carefully at the Continuum Sketch, you will see 'Seeking Help' is at the core of the continuum. This is for the simple reason that your foremost action towards battling depression should be to seek help – be it personal wherein a family member close to you can move in with you to who you can confide in or get medical help wherein a doctor or a certified professional can help you tackle and eventually overcome the ordeals you face. In either case, this 'Help' will be the centrepiece of depression management and treatment and will continue to be a component even when you are implementing the other activities and self-help actions mentioned in the continuum. The accessibility to a live sounding board

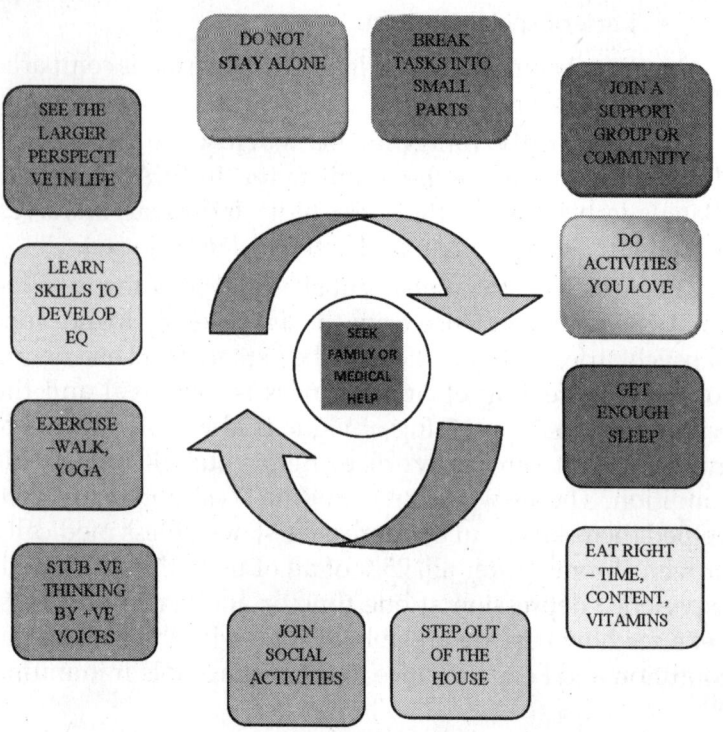

who can reinforce positive actions and thoughts and rectify some aberrations is vital to staying on course with your healing curve. This is also the reason I have put 'Do Not Stay Alone' as a number 1 step in a way.

2. **Break Tasks Into Smaller Parts:** One of the gnawing feelings you must be all too familiar with is the lack of willingness to any work at all. The task could be as simple and routine as taking a bath or cooking a meal. This may partially be due to the lack of motivation and in part due to lack of sustained focus in carrying out any task of medium length. The trick will be breaking a task that seems insurmountable or displeasing to you into smaller do-able activities. So a bath can be broken into a series of activities like:

- Taking a look at your wardrobe to see what you would love to wear for the day.
- Take them and arrange them in the bathroom.
- Take a short break.
- Look into the mirror and admire any one part of your face that you think is attractive - say eyes or nose and want to look after it well.
- Enter the bathroom and cleanse your face.
- Take a short break.
- Take out your favourite bath soap, bath salt, scented bath bubbles, put on relaxing music and step in for the bath.

3. **Join A Support Group:** It is important to be a regular at the support groups for depression. You may ask why we need to do this especially when we already have a supportive family member or a psychologist we are consulting. The answer is because:
   a. The support group meetings and get together provide an outing and thereby an outlet to your emotions outside of the house with people who you think understand you and to who you can speak uninhibitedly to which you may not be able to with the doctor or a family member keeping various attachments and complexities in mind.
   b. It is important to hear what those in situation like you are doing in real time on how to cope with the condition.
   c. It also gives you a larger perspective to life when you see those less fortunate than yourself in the same group and reduces your feeling of isolation being a part of a group.

4. **Do Activities You Love:** There may be activities that you enjoy when you are not depressed or used to before you started to experience depression. Make a list of

those activities. Did you like to watch movies? Did you have a green thumb? When you have it all together at a place, make sure you have what goes into recreating those times and do them when you are feeling low. So the next time you feel listless and do not want to leave the bed to cook or run an errand, think of the music you used to or still enjoy or a new type of music you would like to experiment with. Step out to garden, or go to the theatres, or just visit the mall or buy a few music CDs of a different genre than what you usually listen to, read a book or watch a sitcom on television that you have recorded from old times. Try an old thing the new way. Do a different activity each time. After this you may want to do the chores that are required as you would be more motivated to do them now.

5. **Get Enough Sleep:** Unfortunately depression often includes disturbances in sleep patterns partly emanating from the inadequate levels of serotonin in the system and eventually affecting the amount of melatonin required for sleep. Apart from biological and genetic reasons, there are a host of other reasons that keep patients of depression awake at night or sleeping too much in the day time. It is important that you do all that is necessary to create an atmosphere of sleep before bedtime, avoid the use of caffeine, alcohol, tobacco after sunset, eat light and healthy dinners, avoid reading thrillers and action-packed suspense movies before bed time, keep the lights and music soft. The use of sleeping tablets is <u>not</u> advisable unless you are being supervised by a psychologist or any certified medical professional.

6. **Eat Right- Time, Content, and Vitamins:** A lot of people diagnosed with depression also have unhealthy diets and food habits. They may be eating food that serve as triggers, eating a type of food more than others, not eating food at the right times or serving large portions. Many of the patients are often found deficient in certain

minerals and vitamins that make their condition worse. It is thus important that you watch what you are eating, how much and when. If you think you are headed towards neglecting food or binge-eating to cope with depression, get a close friend or family to monitor it for you. Set out a weekly routine and have it seen that you stick to it. Make sure you eat all your meals using small portions minimizing on sugars and fats, and optimizing intakes of fibres, proteins and complex carbohydrates. In addition include Vitamin B6 and 12 in your diet. Include non-allergy nuts and fish, chicken and avoid red meats, and alcohols. It is alright to indulge in them once a week as a treat to yourself to stay motivated.

7. **Step Out Of The House:** It is very important that you get a change of scenery. No matter how beautiful your home is, it is one you have seen and been in for long hours. A short change – even for the marginally worse will help appreciate the comfort and safety of your home. Boredom is poison for depression. Stepping out at day time will also provide you the much needed sunlight. This is important for the manufacture of serotonin, a critical neurotransmitter that has a major role in mental conditions. Next time you feel low, you would do good to consider stepping out to the open-air theatre or sit at the park benches with your magazine or visit the alfresco tea and curio shops.

8. **Stub Negative Thoughts By Loud Positive Thoughts:** There is a near-consistent chatter that goes on inside of most of us. The chatter is especially negative and self-destructive for those suffering from depression. It harms our confidence in ourselves and blows our resolve at self-help. Over a period of time, we believe what our inner voice has been saying and make realities of the disastrous ends our minds have thought of for us. Luckily there is a proven technique that can serve as an immediate rebuff to negative thoughts. The next time you hear the

inner voice telling you "I don't think I feel like cooking a meal today", you tell it audibly and fairly loudly that you would love the aroma of your favourite recipe XYZ and would love to see the expression on the children's faces if you cook ABC today as a surprise. Repeat this sentence many times and audibly each time for the inner negative voice to be stubbed. Slowly and over a short period of time your negative voice will learn to keep quiet. You could also try stubbing this inner voice by singing or humming your favourite tune immediately on the start of a self-deprecating thought.

9. **Exercise – Walk, Yoga, Breathe– Repeat:** For a person, who does not want much work, wants to stay in bed and feels demotivated, exercising is probably a tall order to make. However, workouts are a potent healer for your condition. Any activity that involves repetitive movements (including chewing during eating!) helps release feel good hormones such as endorphins, dopamine, and serotonin and cleanses out harmful toxins.[18] When you start out, you must keep realistic and small goals like a 10-minute walk or walking the dog in the park and slowly increase it to biking or jogging. Your exercise can take a non-conventional form too – something that you are interested in, able to sustain as a long-term activity and enjoy – like dancing, yoga, pilates, swimming etc. All of these improve your mood, cleanse the body of toxins and improve your cardiovascular condition not to mention improve stamina, flexibility and build up immunity. Exercises also help release the fight-or-flight hormone catecholamines that are precursors to many stimulants in the body. Practice of controlled breathing will provide relaxation in addition to the above benefits.

---

18. You may read details of how exercise helps in my book 'The Urban Woman's Integrated Fitness Guide', Publishers: Hay House India.

10. **Learn Skills To Increase Your E.Q.:** Emotional Intelligence Quotient refers to "the ability, capacity, skill or, in the case of the trait EI model, a self-perceived grand ability to identify, assess, manage and control the emotions of one's self, of others, and of groups."[19] You must remember that each one of us goes through life's trials but each one of us internalises or uses the experience in different ways to arrive at different perspectives and act accordingly. Though the scope of this book does not permit the vast realms of developing Emotional Intelligence skills, you can still look at books and other material including classes that train you in techniques to build up your E.Q. levels. In essence these skills will help you to recognize your stress and reduce it yourself, it will provide you the ability to recognize and manage your emotions desirably, give you the ability to use non-verbal communication, utilisation of humour to tackle challenges and offer the ability to resolve conflict with positive outcomes. As is obvious each of these abilities will help you control your depressive states as per your desire.

11. **Identify Your Triggers:** There will be triggers for any physical, mental or emotional conditions in us. It is for our benefit that we identify them by keeping a log book or a journal where we record the occurrence of the episode of depression and the events that preceded it. For those who experience depression the culprits are often stress, work overload, unrealistic goals, drugs, bad relationships, etc. Whatever your trigger is you will need help keeping a watchful eye on it and ensuring they do not contribute to starting episodes. To keep triggers off your day you will need to:

---

19. Bradberry, Travis and Greaves, Jean. (2009). "Emotional Intelligence 2.0". San Francisco: Publishers Group West. (ISBN 9780974320625)

a. Plan your day and activities ahead setting realistic goals.
b. Provide for the components of the activities a day before.
c. Generate a set of distracting yet interesting components that you can do when craving sets in.

If you find it impossible to keep track of your triggers and get a hold on them, it is advisable you seek medical help.

5. The demons of divorce

Stress, both mental and emotional that emanates from a divorce is ranked by some health journals only next to that which comes from death of a spouse or child and in many cases ranks higher than stress caused by injury, financial crisis or even a jail term. No matter how amicable a separation or divorce is, it tests our emotional seams to the limits. Everyone involved directly and indirectly, but closely, such as, parents and children are equally and sometimes even more affected than us. Divorce seems dispassionate in its preference of how old, famous or rich we are, and it serves as a severe blow to some of us at more than one level.

Amidst all the heartbreak, humiliation and feelings of sorrow, self-pity, anger, anxiety and despair etc., are legal loopholes and financial hassles to overcome. It takes a toll on the mind making us lose appetite, sleep, and interest in work, children, family and our surrounding. Our entire world would feel like being centred on ourselves and we could easily lose sight of our own good. At such times we can drift to being alone and be given to extreme emotions often. The good news is that despite being in such a sticky and undesirable situation, you can do some bare minimum things to help yourself out of this tough time.

You must remember at all times that you must give yourself enough space and sufficient time to grieve the loss of a relationship that was meant to last a lifetime. Though grieving is a complex process and a painful and time

Erasing the Emotional Scars – Tackling the sticky six

consuming one, it is probably the most important one that helps us heal.

Grieving will take the various phases of shock, denial, numbness, anger, despair etc., but you must fight them. It is not healthy and often proves counterproductive to the process of exiting from the past.

At this point it is also important to point that there is no correct time to stop the grieving process. It varies from person to person. However, on an outer limit, you must be able to come to terms with the loss of relationship and start to swing back to life in a year or year and a half's time, beyond which time it is striking negatively at your health and you must seek professional or medical help to help you overcome the divorce or separation.

As with coping with death, there are certain particulars you must ensure you do. These include not taking any impulsive decisions which have long term implications on your life ahead (financial or legal decisions regarding yourself and your children), staying from suicidal thoughts and self-destructive actions by occupying yourself with priority works that need to be attended to – a visit to the lawyer, spending time talking to the children etc., find interests around you, getting help from family or anyone who is willing to serve as an emotional support and physical support for the household, enrolling with support groups, moving house.

During all times be kind to yourself. This is the time you need yourself. You need to not hold yourself responsible for the happening of events. It takes two to tango and some if not more of the damage is always inflicted by the other party. You must thus learn to forgive yourself first. You can help yourself by maintaining a diary of your thoughts and emotions, a strategy of a future course of action broken down into smaller steps, embedding exercises and healthy food into your schedule or any other activity that keeps you healthily and productively occupied. One of the best ways to lessen the pain is to do community work. It goes a long way to benefit your karma and seeing and working with those less fortunate than yourself, opens up new perspectives in life.

In the pages that follow I have chalked out an outline along which you could cruise and help get pointers at how the two most important part of your life can be handled during a separation or divorce – your children and you. The outline is a sketchy or rudimentary one, yet it will give you an idea of the flow you should take in the event of a divorce. Of course, the best plan will be the one you draw yourself keeping the specifics of your household and life in particular incorporated to the outlines I have thus given.

Mentor Your Mind

1. Supporting and helping your child/children out of the messy times:

Divorce of parents will mean and be viewed very differently by a child than it will be for the parent though at some level both may be insecure about similar issues. For a child it means loss of the life they are used to in terms of financial or physical comforts. It may also mean deprivation of having physical access to both parents at the same time. If these issues were not enough for a child, there will be a hundred questions that arise in their minds. Their questions will be about their own future, possible change of school, change of residence, living with a relation for a specified time period, questions that deal with trust issues as well as jealousy with friends with undisturbed homes, taking sides or even coming to terms with their own emotions at such a time. You must realize that they are as affected if not more by the unfolding of divorce events. However, there are ways in which you can minimize the blow on them. Here's help on how you can:

Listening to what the children are telling and what they are not is vital and provides many clues that will help you help them. Your child/children could be looking for both the parent's inclusion and involvement in vital and not so vital decisions of their lives; they could be looking for assurance of present and future peace especially when the family is together as well as looking for ease of conversation and a surety for continued love from both of you. In case there is verbal or implied hint of any of these, you must take care that it is addressed and preferably to allay the fears or the

EMOTIONAL ASSURANCE

Tell them you love them repeatedly
    Respect their feelings/emotions
        Be physically and emotionally close
            Promote honesty
                Listen to what they say

VERBAL ASSURANCE

Tell them the truth
    Talk about the changes
        Assure they'll be alright
            Be honest
                Parent present

discomfort of the child. It will go a long way in easing your own life and conscience.

It is equally important that to be able to communicate effectively at the time you and spouse are both around the child at the same to be able to decide on future matters, both of you decide beforehand to practice restraint. This means avoid blaming, name calling and other such things that will jeopardise the issue at hand that needs discussing and also make it very difficult for the child who witnesses this to trust both of you and/or listen to what you preach later. You must make sure that you and your spouse who are now heading in separate directions present a united front when together with the child. It will also signal to the child that both the parents will be there for him/her when things go wrong setting their own differences aside.

Though you will always be the best judge of how to handle the dreadful turmoil divorce brings, you must remember at all times that you are doing the best in the present circumstances and to the best of your abilities regardless of the outcomes that develop out of your actions or decisions. Be more forgiving towards your own self. This way you will be less likely to misdirect your negativity to your children. A good way to set children into a supported state of being is by giving them a routine to follow reflecting stability of sorts. This will help you and your dear dependents to hold on to something solid in a time of undesirable changes in their lives.

2. Supporting yourself through a divorce:

As if going through the demons of a divorce is not enough what with the emotional, mental and physical scars they leave upon us if uncared for, we often also have to take care of others such as a child or an ageing or ailing parent. To be able to go through this process with as much ease as is reasonable to expect from out of such a time, it is important if not imperative that you keep yourself the focus of your life. Remember, if you fall prey to the evils stress brings in such times, you will be doing injustice to yourself first and those around you. It is a time when you must make time for yourself at least every other day if not every day.

Pampering Yourself Emotionally

i. Let yourself feel the despair, sorrow, fear, anger or any other emotion in the short and medium run.
ii. Contact a close friend or a trusted family member with who you can talk freely about what you feel.
iii. Hug yourself often, love and forgive yourself regardless of who is the more culpable individual in the divorce proceedings.
iv. See if you can take outside or professional help with respect to talking it over and helping you out of the mess emotionally.
v. Remember to inch ahead every week progressing towards a brighter or at least a lighter future.
vi. Keep negativity out by occupying yourself with activities such as visiting the salon or developing a hobby like gardening or working out etc.

Pampering Yourself Physically

i. Eat well, eat frequently in small portions including healthy foods. It is alright to crave for comfort foods at such a time but be wary of the amounts of sweet treats and fried foods you are taking in.
ii. Build a list of things you can do to keep yourself productively distracted from wallowing in self-pity. Do at least 2 things from that list every day.
iii. If you see or are pointed out by someone close that you are falling in the trap of alcohol and drugs to seek comfort, you must immediately seek professional help to counter this dependence pattern.

iv. Go out on weekends to see the museum, sit at parks, visit historical sites, drop in on old friends, make new ones, visit malls, etc. Any activity that keeps you distracted. You can take your loved ones along with you so that it will be a change for everyone concerned.
v. Take time to exercise and enrol into confidence building and restoration classes.
vi. Keep albums and letters etc. that remind you of old times with your spouse away.
vii. Build a new hobby – environmental or health related hobbies are great as are skill development ones.
viii. Redo your bedroom or your wardrobe.

However you plan to work it out building a routine, having your close friend or family at hand, keeping perspective of a better future and remaining healthy and cultivating healthy distractions will go a long way to ease the pain of the emotional upheaval that any divorce or separation brings along with itself.

6. Work-life balance

Losing the 'desired' equilibrium between work that is necessary to earn a living and work that is necessary to live a life is a phenomenon that has gained note in hospitals and health care clinics since the last two decades. There is a reason why I use the word 'desired'. This is because it is neither realistic nor necessary to spend equal number of hours at work and at home (or a place which is desirable and non-work). As long as the tip of the scale brings out healthy outcomes or set of consequences, you could say your work-life is in balance. So it is a fluid term and varies within a range for each one of us and may even differ in the different phases of life for the same person. Think about it.

Keeping with the rising cost of living and the more current global recession an increasing number of the working force is falling prey to the evils of long working hours and more working days a week. Steven L. Sauter, chief of the Applied Psychology and Ergonomics Branch of the National Institute for Occupational Safety and Health in Cincinnati, Ohio, pointed out that recent studies show that "the workplace has become the single greatest source of stress". Corroborating this finding, Michael Feuerstein, professor of clinical psychology at the Uniformed Services University of the Health Sciences at Bethesda Naval Hospital has categorically stated, "We're seeing a greater increase in work-related neuro-skeletal disorders from a combination of stress and ergonomic stressors".

So why is it so difficult to prioritize what is important and what is not for the otherwise intelligent person? The answers are not so basic or simple and could lie in any number of reasons such as job insecurity, financial uncertainty, rising cost of living, increasing standards of living, trying to keep away from a tense home, obsessive behavior, lack of social life etc. In the end a person with a distorted work-life balance will experience health concerns that could range from immune system weakness, cardiovascular conditions, fatigue, migraines, back, wrist, eyes and neck problems, loss of focus and unhealthy diet along with sedate living.

Think about it, you work because you want to be able to afford good living and if situation arises, be able to pay the medical bills. Ironically, with an unbalanced work schedule, you end up mounting your medical bills when you are ill with overwork. You want to be able to live a grand life, but are actually spending all hours in indoor pollution of your office. Both men and women are equally affected by work stress and in turn it disturbs the equilibrium of their families – children and older parents.

A work to non-work ratio should bring about the experiencing of a sense of peace, contentment, pride, enjoyment, health and achievement factors in your life. If it is able to do this for you and most of your family members who you live with – then despite your long or short hours at work, your work-life is probably balanced.

So how can you tell your work-life balance is askew? Here are a few pointers:

- You feel easily irritable at home after work hours.
- You wake up in the morning stressed about completing home work to rush to office.
- You end up thinking of pending office work during the quality-time at home.
- You have no energy left to contribute things of value after your return from office.
- You have no social circle outside of colleagues you see over work hours.
- You no longer have any real hobbies and interests except peering into the office laptop, or receiving office calls from subordinates and being available on a Blackberry.

If any of those observations sounds like you and your spouse is pointing to it or children are complaining about you not spending enough time with them, your work-life schedule is probably upset.

Though it is realistic to expect our work-life balance to go out of sync for short and definite periods of time – like when financial books are closing at year end at office or it is budgeting time at your workplace or other similar high activity level period, but beyond these few or every other month highs there should be a predictable time schedule for you. Yet if you are fire-fighting every day or week to keep a balance between work and home chores, you could look at a few suggestions of how you could help yourself, your family and eventually your work.

Erasing the Emotional Scars – Tackling the sticky six 121

How To Read The Table Below:

There are some observations you would have made about your the pace, load and spread of your own life - both from the point of office or business work and life at home. These are outlined under the column 'Observation'. These are 'problem areas'.

The Checks column briefly sketches what you could do to work towards a solution for the 'problem' (or Observation).

Thus every Observation will have a set of Checks OR every problem will have a set of actions you can execute at your level to overcome the problems.

The Comments column will have my thoughts for the problem-solution set. Here, I may have put forth a supportive-suggestion or some new auxiliary actions to do. It could also be pointing at the arrival of a solution in this column. In other words, this column helps to take your understanding a step further in terms of problem-action-solution format. Some comment boxes could be blanks as no further inputs are required for that particular problem-action-solution set.

Observation	Checks	Comments
• Your life looks over-crowded with work and respon-sibilities.	• Make an input list of the 5 things you most value. • Make an input list of 3 things you would most like to focus on right now. • Make an output list with entries common to list 1 and 2 (such as children, health, hobby etc.)	• This is what is your core value list with which you work.

Observation	Checks	Comments
• Your boss asks you to come to office over weekends more out of routine than call of work or because it is expected out of workers.	• If you will not respect your personal time, nobody will. Ask what exactly you need to do and then chart to fit it over the week. • Go if it is urgent. • Remain available to your office on email and cell on only specific time window. • Make sure you are not late on deliverables during the week. • Use technology cleverly to your advantage to save time.	• Numbers of work hours logged does not mean you are smart, it may point otherwise.
• You are not able to cope with a flurry of outside and inside work pressures that you envisage staying for the next 3 months.	• Seek help – get a family member like mum or dad or an old relative to pitch in for that time. • Get professional help to help at home or talk to a life coach to sort out the temporary but sticky situation.	• Talk to the family taking everybody including the children in, so that they may understand the plan and why it is being done.
• You feel as though you are stuck in a rut and want to take some time off.	• Chart out one new place to see or visit every day of the weekend – museum, park, theatre, mall, historical site etc. Check with your children so that they may come at least one of the 2 days out with you. They may have some new places to recommend. • Take time out together at home for activities – gardening, compost pit, craft work, watching movies.	• You do not have to take a vacation to a faraway place if your work wants you on site – you can plan fun and relaxation in your city. • If you do not wish to have the children around or they are too young, you can arrange a babysitter for the time you are out.

Erasing the Emotional Scars – Tackling the sticky six

Observation	Checks	Comments
• The weekend is approaching and your planner looks overflowing with office work, pending personal work and home chores.	• Make a list of work that is priority and stick to them first. • Next attempt B category work which are desirable to do for everyone's benefit and attend to them on Day 2 of the weekend. The rest can probably wait for another time.	• On such occasions, be wary of spending too much time surfing the internet and watching television. They eat away at your time so subtly and effectively that it is hard to realize when it is happening and keeps you away from what matters.
• Your friends/colleagues have made a habit of hanging out post work every Friday at cafes and pubs and though you have gone a few times, you don't feel up to it every time.	• Learn to say 'No'. It does not have to be rude, it can be done politely. • Do not take their push or jabs at you personally or make you feel bad. • You can tell them the truth politely or if you'd rather not, you can always fib about some work or home job that needs attending to.	• However, you can go the times you wish to for a change. • You must not feel compelled to either go all the time or not go all the time. Play as per your mood and feelings.
• The pile up of work at home and office is making you slip on things.	• Use time management tips such as using organisers and reminders, alarms etc. You can also use post-it chits and mark dates on calendars to make it easy for you.	

Observation	Checks	Comments
• You are looking for some free time and have none – leaving you resentful.	• Pamper yourself with private time such as a visit to the manicurist, pedicurist, spa or massage centre or simply alone cafe time or walking through the malls. • You can join yoga or glass painting, pottery or candle making or baking classes or any other thing that interests and enlivens you. • Get enough rest and eat well.	• If you do not wish to have the children around or they are too young, you can arrange a babysitter for the time you are out. • You can eat out and have something packed for back home so that it serves as an off from the kitchen as well.
• You find yourself helpless any time there is a shift in work volume at home or at work.	• Build a network with colleagues who can cover for you when you are out of office or friends who can pitch in an emergency situation at home. • Enlist with a trusted and certified day care whose services you can avail if need be. • Sign into community service volunteers who can pitch in for you at home front in emergent cases.	• Networking with colleagues and friends should be strong. • You must meet or speak with them often. • Be ready to pay in cash or kind to appreciate for the services rendered.

The Way Forward

The previous pages took us through some of the most reported, recorded and tabulated emotional states (with hospitals and caregivers) that make us feel helpless and unstable and are unpleasant experiences for the sufferer. Though there are logical and easy-to-comprehend ways to tackle those emotional disturbances, they are in essence 'band-aid' approach to a problem. It is important that we think long-term beyond the fire fighting approach.

From the 'life as a whole' perspective, we need to pave inroads unto ourselves so that we are able to move forward from these agonizing experiences and states to one where equilibrium is easy to reach, if not maintain at most times. Obvious as this may sound, it is far from simple and some of the steps will take courage to go through not to mention months or even years to cultivate as a matter of habit. In the following content, I have put forth for you the basic 4-step approach that will help you build a lifetime of self-support through development of inner strength and developing a 'nose' for what is right thing to do or think.

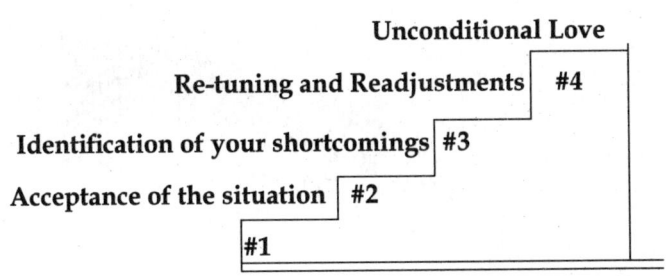

The 4-Step Evolution To Quick Return To Emotional Stability

1. Acceptance of the situation

This acceptance does not mean resignation to the situation. In fact, it is quite the opposite. This acceptance refers to the non-judgemental acceptance without resistance of the prevailing situation. This sort of acceptance is creative and causes us to take progressive and proactive course for a desirable future.

This acceptance is the acknowledgment of the circumstance in which you find yourself, whether controllable or not. It does not belong to the realms of acceptance of yourself as a person, acceptance of yourself as perceived by others, which are essentially outcomes of unconditional love for oneself. This stage comes a little later in the scheme of things. To be able to get to that or any other phase, you will need to accept where we are in the way we are. As a result of this acknowledgment, you will be able to make sensible plans to foray ahead with your life with constructive ideas about how to make life better.

That said, acceptance does not come easy. After all, each one of us would desire things to go as per our plans and desires. Yet many times they do not. If the factors that lay the plans asunder are controllable, we take another route or try and include them so that we achieve our desired outcome. But if the causal factors are beyond our control, we have little option but to either accept the situation with personal clarity and awareness or perish. This acceptance provides a practical and productive alternative to a closed door or a 'No Way Out' situation. It is an acceptance to Change.

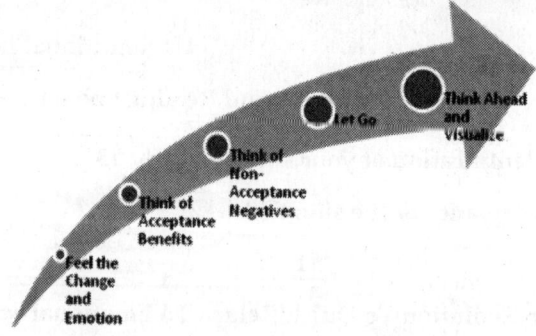

Ricochet Ahead With Acceptance

a. Feel the Change and Emotion:

It is crucial that you go through the emotions that come to you at the onset of the change that you wish to accept. The emotions may be of despair and helplessness, anger and frustration. They are all valid emotions. To be able to go further ahead with our life, it is important to feel and live out all the emotions especially the negative ones, so that they are not pent up. Only when we are clear of negative feelings will we have made space for positivity and constructive behaviour. Be in that present moment and cry or talk to yourself if you feel like it. You may do it alone or seek a family or a friend's help. Seeking professional help is just as good. At this early stage, there is no need to seek approval for your emotional bouts.

b. Think of the Acceptance Benefits:

It is important that as the splurge of emotions start to reduce in a month or two's time, you start to deliberately and consciously start to move towards positive emotions. If at this stage you continue to linger on to crippling emotions, you are likely to go into chronic depression and possibly self-destructive behaviour with a longer recovery. Thus it is imperative that you will yourself to think of the benefits that will arise in your life when you move forward, the benefits you enjoyed leading a normal life which will be great to have again – different but normal. Think of the little joys in stepping out again, enjoying normal health like better sleep cycles and appetite, meeting friends, going to the malls, joining work, classes, etc.

c. Think of the Non-Acceptance Negatives:

During this time, it is also suggested that you think of the situations that will prevail if you do not accept change that has occurred in your life. By non-acceptance, I mean, resisting the change. You may go over the episode or incident or past years over and over again and feel drained of energy and motivation to do what is required of you to live better and more fully. You may suffer debilitating physical ailments like heart conditions, asthma, hypertension, stress-induced diabetes as well as mental ailments such as depression etc. Think of all those loved ones around you and how they will be affected. Think of how work and your finances will be affected with resistance, rumination, negative comparisons on what could have been etc. This will motivate you to come out of the situation by accepting and looking forward to the benefits more readily.

d. Let Go:

The process of letting go can be either painful or painless depending upon the time you have spent or degree of cleansing you have done, thought you have put and your mental and emotional readiness to move ahead. It is a factor of Steps a–c. Letting go can be aided by meditation and controlled breathing exercises. It can be assisted by community service and *seva*.

e. Think Ahead and Visualize:

Spend some solitary time visualizing the life you want now for yourself and those who live with you. Do this every day. Write it down in a diary or speak to yourself about it – not in a complaining negative way but as though you are looking forward to it and are taking steps to move towards it little every day. Visualization is a powerful tool in healing and also for moving ahead positively and practically through tough situations in life.

2. Identification of your shortcomings and working a plan

Poet Brendan Francis told us, 'Once we accept our limits, we go beyond them.' This is probably one of the toughest exercises ranking just below acceptance of the situation. It is hard to see yourself with shortcomings for two simple reasons. We are living in the situation, so it is difficult to see ourselves from a neutral and outside perspective. We are too involved and close to the situation and suffering from it. This accompanied with the fact that it is hard for us to accept our own shortcomings as it is an almost direct admission of our deficiencies or inadequacies etc. In a way and during such situations, we are generally in states of moderate to acute denial.

However, unless we identify our shortcomings ourselves, we will be less willing to take the road to corrective action. When identification of failings is done by someone else other than us, we are less likely to be cohesive with our approach to re-establishing equilibrium.

The exercise of pointing out where we need to fix ourselves is not to implicate ourselves but to get us out of our condition. This makes regular self-examination an important starting point for all of us. Here are a few steps you will need to take to make progress with yourself:

A step by step approach to identification of foible points

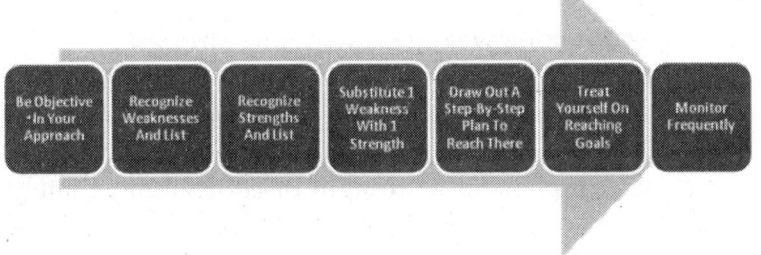

a. Be objective in your approach:

Our evaluation and identification has to be unbiased and knowledgeable to get an accurate picture of where we can plug in the loopholes in ourselves. If we are untrue in this process, we would be fooling no one but ourselves. We would also be building a plan inconsistent with our shortcomings and thus not getting the result we want from the exercise.

b. Recognize weaknesses and list:

The listing of weaknesses is the real first step in our progress and though we need not be overly zealous in going all out with the slightest negatives, we must be brutally honest with the ones which are our real concerns. Our weakness list may include list of resources we lack in terms of friends, information, money, etc., or our own attributes such as introverted, sensitive nature or an aggressive temperament, or even emotional concerns involving image issues etc. Make a list of them. A meaningful list will usually not have more than 4-5 items.

c. Recognize strengths and list:

Just as we have indicated our weakness, we need to make a listing of our strengths. This list can be a bit more liberal in terms of chalking out even those which are marginal strong points. So we could have strengths such as ability or passion for writing or singing, painting, reading or have a good sense of humour or a strong will power, a good health and physical features, a compassionate nature etc. Include them all.

d. Substitute one weakness with one strength:

Take your most urgently attention-requiring weakness and see if you can substitute it with any of the first three strengths. It should be possible. Every time you hit the weakness on your path, implement a strength of choice immediately in its place so that it is visible and audible to you and serves as a reinforcement of the improvement process. As time progresses and you are able to replace the most dire weaknesses successfully, you could move on down in your list with substitutions of other shortcomings.

e. Draw out a step-by-step plan to reach there:

Chalking out a daily schedule that involves reinforcements, motivation, implementations, personal time, work, healthy eating, workouts, meditation, doing evaluation lists and the like will be integral to getting to your end goal. It gives a day-to-day and minute perspective to your progress.

f. Treat yourself on reaching goals:

This is a form of reinforcement of the 'good' in yourself and the success and thereby belief in yourself and the plan. All small objectives and goals on the way to the milestones should be appreciated and celebrated. This would also go a long way to provide the much needed motivation to keep on at the difficult track.

g. Monitor frequently:

Monitoring helps us evaluate and reassess some of the minor and major progresses and deficiencies in our plan as well as in its implementation, assumptions and results. Once we move on to the next phase of our plan, we must go back to frequently re-test what we have achieved in the previous phases to keep the lessons alive.

3. Re-tuning

We need to re-tune and re-adjust because:

- We along with the environment in which we live are constantly in a state of flux.
- We need to take action on the prior step of monitoring and reviewing our performance.

When we find aberrations, we need to address them to stay on track. We can address them by:

- Changing our actions and thoughts or,
- Moving the goal a little to the front or back or,
- Fine-tuning our resources such as time and fund availability that the scheme may demand.

You may require re-visiting the various aspects such as:

- 'Do I need to be gentler in relationships with family and work?'
- 'Do I need to set realistic mini goals, keeping the big goal in picture?'

You'll need to rework these areas one at a time. This is a critical juncture or point in your self-mentoring. If you do not give it the attention it requires, you could be doing all the things and not quite reaching where you intended to in the time you intended to. Effective goal actualisation is possible only when new goals which align with the new situation are made possible. This ensures both the process and the goal to be relevant, motivational and most importantly survive the transition from thought, to action, through to completion.

4. Unconditional love

This is the part that involves acceptance of the self. Unless we are able to accept ourselves with all the foibles, strengths and in all the colours, we will not be able to forge ahead successfully. Our progress will be short-lived and dotted with frequent self-doubt and repetitions of old emotional and behavioural patterns. For this forgiveness and faith in oneself is of critical value. Because these things are hard to arrive at, they take time to achieve and are learnt from the lessons through stages 1-3 discussed earlier. I believe this is also the last stage of letting go of a set of old debilitating habits, patterns and dysfunctional values to be able to move forward and on with life.

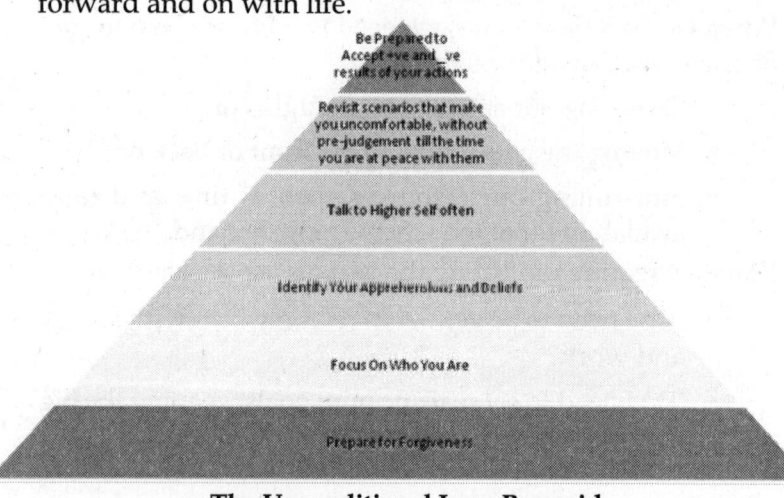

The Unconditional Love Pyramid

a. Prepare for forgiveness:

Preparing for forgiveness essentially means starting on a clean slate with no prior writings and self-images. In other words we must drop our prior notions and expectations from ourselves. Clearly the old standards are now redundant and even harmful and it is now time to let go off them. It is equally important that besides starting on a non-judgemental note, we also free ourselves from the strain of consciousness of how others perceive us. Basically we need to be free from putting any unnecessary and unproductive demands upon ourselves so that we can focus on our way forward. This way we will be able to forgive ourselves for all our past – both attributes and reactions.

b. Focus on who you are:

Once we have prepared the grounds for moving on, we must concentrate on the pivot person – us. This means we should see ourselves as we truly are. We are people who are living the learning process. See yourself as a living embodiment with values, work, emotions and one surrounded by loved ones or family. See yourself as someone who is willing to learn, experiment and take risks to move ahead regardless of the temporary setbacks you may face in the process. Through this entire process keep the focus on yourself – keep yourself first.

c. Identify your apprehensions and beliefs:

Once you are able to focus on yourself, you will observe that you are clearly able to identify your apprehensions and beliefs. These will be new founded ones and will amongst others have experiences drawn from what has only just occurred in your life. Stay with them and see them objectively time and again.

d. Talk to your higher self:

Set yourself patches of 'alone or me' time. This is the time you take to address those issues you identified in the earlier step with your higher self or the inner consciousness. When you talk to your inner self, remember just stating your issues will do. You need not state anything beyond such as undertones of emotions etc. Your higher self hears you and will process that information even while you are not aware of it. It often comes up with solutions. Wait for the solutions. If you are tuned in, you will find them.

e. Revisit discomfort zones:

Much as this sounds counter-productive it is actually a part of deeper and total healing. To be able to get over the past experiences and accept the current situation and emotions you will need to be comfortable with what has unfolded in the past. You cannot move to the future effectively and healthily if we are carrying the burden of past discomfort. This will be an unpleasant process and you will take several attempts and some time before you become indifferent or at best comfortable with the past.

f. Accept any outcome of your actions:

Any life's learning and subsequent personal advancement is ineffectual and false if we are scared to face results. Results may be to an extent beyond our control. We may be able to control it only to the extent they are dependent directly on our actions. In either one case, we must be prepared to face them. A negative outcome of our decision should be used as a learning and lesson and treated just as valuable as a positive outcome which can be used as a motivation and reinforcement for success of the learning and moving ahead.

Living in Emotional Wellness

Having read the preceding pages gives us an idea of why it is almost as important to keep well emotionally as it is to keep fit physically or mentally. Cases are rife of people with healthy and active lifestyles succumbing to heart attacks and cancers. If you take a holistic perspective, you will be able to trace back their end to mental stress, unattended emotional issues like suppressed anger, feeling of not being loved, not being able to forgive or accept etc., that ate into their bodies despite having followed an exercise regimen.

Though I have addressed some of the issues that come into prominence repeatedly in the media and in our own lives of families of friends and colleagues, there are those which the scope of this book does not permit and hence are not touched upon. Yet they are significant issues such as eating disorders and certain behavioural or personality disorders that actually come more under the address and focus of medical community first and thus should not be tackled here with a self-help approach due to their serious nature. They must be seen to by the doctors at the earliest signs of disorder and disequilibrium.

Moving on in our search for emotional wellness, let us take a look at what we can and should do to keep us emotionally healthy. These ideas can be put to practice at any point in your life whether you are experiencing any emotional ill-health or not. These tools and practices can be fit into our daily lives in any time slot that is free and available to us. If we lead tremendously busy lives, we must make time for them. Neglecting them as we have seen takes a heavy toll in more ways than one and often sneaks in so stealthily that we do not notice the build up to a breakdown. I also recommend that those with fairly busy lives can 'live out' any one of the various tools chalked out below each day. This way, they do not have to repeat themselves, escape boredom and get to do all the activities in a week. People will also do good to set time aside for them only over the weekend. However, it is preferable to do one of them each day. We stress and go through a gamut of emotions that stifle us each day and so a daily cleansing routine would be advised.

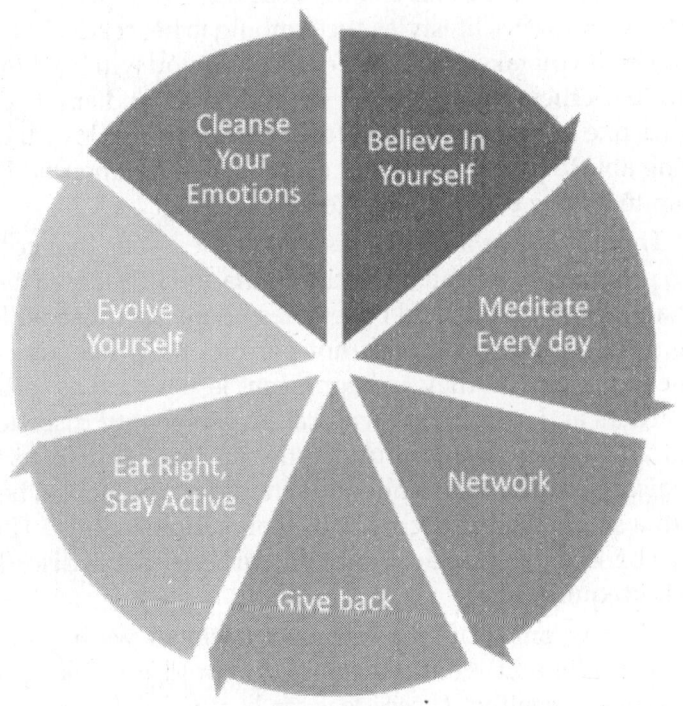

Moving On In Emotional Wellness

a. Believe in yourself:

Make this faith a part of your daily living. Believe in what you do, say, act or decide. Hear what you are doing, see what you are doing and have faith in the action and thought. If you need to hear yourself, say it out audibly for your subconscious to hear and believe it. Say, "I am doing right. God will make this right." Say, "God loves me and I am safe with him." This way faith and belief and God and yourself will bring you comfort and give you the much needed confidence in yourself and your decisions. It will also cut out on negative inner chatter that goes on with each one of us. Stand in front of your home or bathroom mirror and repeat this to yourself. When you do this for a month over and over again, it becomes a reality and you will truly have faith and love unto yourself. It is imperative that you understand that you are the boss of what goes on in your head, and emotions and thoughts are controllable, to be able to make any worthwhile progress.

b. Meditate everyday:

Make ten minutes off your schedule, even if it is at the end of the day to sit in a place and get in touch with your real self. Hear and feel your inner voices and learn what they are telling. Familiarize yourself with this voice and guide. When you sit quietly in a place and reduce body movements and retract from other noises around, you will be able to 'watch' your thoughts and emotions flit past just as an outsider would. This will open your eyes to the temporary nature of thoughts and emotions, feelings, etc., and will make you feel more liberated from their chains. Meditation will bring out your true nature of love, compassion, patience and silence – all the traits required to be rooted to yourself and reality and being strong. You can learn meditation from tapes where you are guided through the steps or from a group meditation class taken by a certified instructor.

c. Network:

When I say network, I mean making a web of people in who you see an embodiment of the traits you would like to acquire. Make friends with those who are kind and are involved in community service and charity work. You can befriend people who are patient such as nurses and other health caregivers and teachers etc. You would know where to find such people. They could be found in group for like-minded people, health centres, old age homes and orphanages or on the internet, in your residing community etc. Network does not mean meeting people from your own profession and industry, or adding another head count to a number base or include a friend whose hobby is shopping or investing in real estate only. Just as you should choose your thoughts, you must be very careful in who you spend non-family and work time with. They affect our thoughts and energy levels the most. Be polite but clear to negative people that you will not have them in your circle for they will bring your thoughts, energy and emotion down with their own.

d. Give back:

Give back to the community from which you have taken. This is a call to charity and community service, which will be discussed in more detail in the last section of the book. Giving back is very nourishing to the soul and has very strengthening and calming effect on us. Charity does not have to involve donations of cash only – they can be of kind such as of food, clothes, books, toys and they could be of the most invaluable knowledge/teaching or of love and care. Community service will connect you to yourself and it will make your meditations easier.

e. Eat right, stay active:

Needless to say, you need to be physically fit to be able to stay emotionally well. It would be a little ambitious to expect a situation where a person is suffering from cardiovascular conditions and think that they are not stressed about it or feel anxious about it. What I mean to say is that, we should eat a nutritive, balanced diet and exercise. With new theories on food and exercise emerging every day, it is impossible to keep up with new trends. Some information also contradicts the older ones, which seemed to have worked for generations. It is ideal to take the middle path without swinging into extremes. There is such a paradox as too much of a good thing doing harm. As long as you eat naturally grown or local produce, eat moderate amounts of white meats and keep to fibres and walk briskly everyday for half an hour, you should see yourself as trouble free without injuries. I am assuming that you do not have a condition to start with. In essence avoid frequent eating of junk food, food with artificial flavours, synthetic drinks, oily and fatty foods, red meats and alcohol and over-exercising or leading a sedate life.

f. Evolve yourself:

Develop skills that will help you grow as a person. Learning new skills keeps the brain functionally young and emotionally contended. Take up activities you always wanted to learn or see yourself turning into your livelihood later. You can either enrol into a brick and mortar class or buy a book to learn it or even join e-classes for it. It will stave off boredom, keep you thinking, forming new neuron connections in the head and keep you mentally and emotionally occupied constructively. You may improve yourself on a variety of levels such as physical, emotional, mental and spiritual depending on the type of activity you have chosen to learn. It will provide a plate of something new to look forward to in your otherwise full and known day.

g. Cleanse your emotions:

We go through a range of emotions every day. They could be of momentary or non-momentary nature. They could be emotions of fear, happiness, sadness, empathy, compassion, anxiety etc. We veil emotions for a variety of reasons such as our surroundings, appropriateness, non-willingness to display our vulnerability to others etc. Whatever be the reason, they are pent up and are suppressed. Over a period of time, if they are left unattended to, give out warning signals in the form of hypertension, irritability. The problem lies deeper and requires emotional detoxification. Not forgiving people and situations of the past has known to lead to cancers of different types. It is thus important that you expunge your emotions each day that day itself. Take the 5 minutes and cry the tears you suppressed on your way to office when you saw a disabled child beg or shout out loud the anger you suppressed when your boss told you were not entitled for a leave you know you need to take.

Yes, it will be a long journey, one that will have to be made a part of your life. Expect to err, but be prepared to regain your stance and learn again. We are all students of life and the business of living is a tough one. Take the lessons not the emotions from your mistakes to be able to come out stronger.

SPIRITUAL FITNESS

"Silence is the goal of all answers. If an answer does not silence the mind, it is no answer."

Sri Sri Ravi Shankar (1956)
Spiritual Guru

Spirituality in Cyber Age

Spirituality has probably been the most misunderstood and debated topic with the world intelligentsia. Every well-defined religion has its own perspective and explanation for its followers. To some, spirituality would mean developing a personal relation with the divine through prayers, to others it would mean reading their holy scriptures, and to some others it would suggest giving alms to the needy or cultivating a sense of neutrality to worldly charms. Almost all these outlooks involve 'religion' to some extent.

To most of us, the word 'spirituality' still conjures up images of austere monks deep in group-meditation in a secluded monastery. How far are these images pertinent in the modern context?

Today, little of these definitions hold relevant in their entirety though their essence still remains as valid. In its essence, almost all religions have a similar scope of the term 'spirituality'. It involves going beyond fending the needs of the physical self and looking for attainment of a 'state of mind' or spirit which go beyond the perceptions of the five senses and satisfy the inner or deeper meaning of our life and its purpose. In other words, Spirituality is the route practiced by the Body and Mind/Intellect to enrich the Soul.

Why should you be spiritually fit?

Any activity that serves a larger cause and goes beyond the immediate goal of serving us makes us feel content at a deeper level. This deep level is hard to define and yet we know it exists because we easily feel it. The feeling of contentment or being alive has been proven scientifically to benefit us.

For long, mainstream sciences have denied the benefits derived from spiritual practices and activities. Only now a few medical and research institutions across the globe have admitted and acknowledged of its merits and contributions towards healing of diseases such as cardiac-arrest oriented paralysis, cancer, dialysis, etc. A case in point is the induction of the Art Of Living Foundation's renowned Sudarshan Kriya Yoga for its patients by the Cardiology Department of All India Institute of Medical Sciences (AIIMS), New Delhi[20].

Some of the other benefits derived from keeping spiritually healthy are:

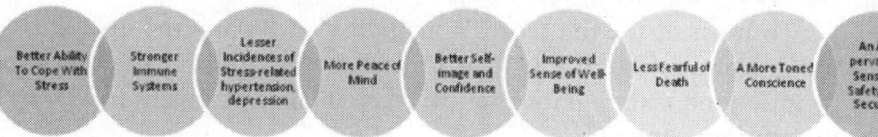

The search for values

Each one of us has two sets of values. One that we are raised or brought up with, i.e., inherited values of our parents which have been imbibed and the second set are the acquired values, i.e., those that are gained from our own life experiences in the process of growing and living. As you may already be familiar our values also change with the passage of time. The values for a teenager will be different from the same person's

---

20. http://timesofindia.indiatimes.com/city/delhi/Yoga-helps-fight-cancer-AIIMS/articleshow/187207.cms
http://www.liebertonline.com/doi/abs/10.1089/acm.2005.11.711
http://www.hvk.org/articles/0208/184.html

value twenty years on. Then of course, there are values for those you love and are close to and those who form your middle and outer circle of friends. In a way, this is important. It helps us demarcate parts of our life into sections that are easy to manage and comprehend. At the same time the values in our basket also clash and clatter seeming to set us back rather than promote our rooting.

There is a chain of evolution even in the value system that exists in the world and generally if one strives in the right direction, the flow into the next level is easy. You will often have noted/experienced that personal or individual values – either inherited or acquired will keep you within the gambit of superficial to sub-superficial levels of existence. They include individual values, such as, honesty, excellence, attractiveness, etc. They are necessary to have, but keep you at a level of preservation. They create and reinforce the illusion of duality and keep us frustrated at the single level.

On the other hand are human values - those that have a broader perspective, such as, compassion for the needy, trust, involvement, support, etc., help us evolve to serve a larger cause and gives us the knowledge of non-dual concepts. These human values may be used as the route to attain the higher goal of spiritual values.

In essence, the ladder of value development will look like this for most of us.

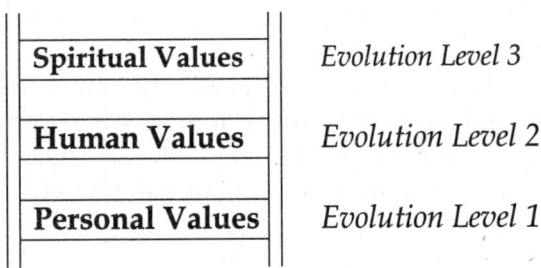

The Ladder of Spiritual Development

There are about a hundred different and positive values – both personal and human. I have made a quick list of thirty common ones most of us aspire to achieve through inculcation and implementation. Check to see how many of these you aspire to have. I say 'aspire' as all values are a lifetime's practice.

Affection	Growth	Pleasure
Compassion	Helping society	Resolve
Competence	Honesty	Restraint
Contentment	Humour	Sacrifice
Ethical practice	Involvement	Strength
Excellence	Knowledge	Support
Fame	Loyalty	Tranquillity
Fearlessness	Money	Trust
Freedom	Patience	Truth
Gratitude	Personal Development	Wisdom

The question of tools and techniques may have occurred to you by now. Yes, there are methods by whose perseverance you will progress from your present state of value-evolution to the next level. However, you must keep in mind that these tools and techniques will form a way of life for you. This is to mean that you will practice them at all times unlike an office job. You will put those tools and means to test and implement them inside and outside your home with consistency.

By consistency is meant non-duality in this case. Let us take an example. Assuming you aspire for ethical practice, you will be as ethical as is possible at office. This could include amongst others reporting on time, planning your work realistically, delegating and executing it diligently and also be prepared for feedback from the client and the supervisor. Outside of office, it may mean being honest with your family and non-family commitments. That is to say, you should tell a guest who plans to drop in late in the evening that you are tired and would love to keep it at another time when you both enjoy the meeting instead of telling her that you are busy with your child's assignments and co-curricular commitments.

It also means that if you are involved with community work and say, are in-charge of the funds – you must be honest in your dealings, recording, allocating funds in the most transparent ways. It could also mean that you should be upfront about why you will be able to attend only certain days of the week, though politely. Practicing such ethical conduct through honesty will then become the pivot around which living will revolve irrespective of people's lack of fondness to such demeanour, though you will maintain politeness at all times. It will be a personal journey and a commitment unto you.

Take the 5-minute questionnaire and scale where you stand today. Think where you would like to be in half a decade from now and unfold the journey. As D. Williams put it, "Before you have practiced, the theory is useless; after you have practiced, the theory is obvious."

The 5-minutes towards self-observation – a questionnaire

Think of how much time you spend on thinking about yourself at a deeper level than superficial existence in a day. I say 'superficial existence' not because they are not necessary, because some of them are. But our thoughts about ourselves usually revolve around which foods to eat or clothes to wear, which creams suit our skin or shampoo our hair. And though these are important for self-preservation, they are still at a rudimentary level of existence. They skim through only the top layer of our lives and living.

The other dimension is of looking outwards. We dedicate a major chunk of the day in addressing, tackling and managing issues that may not directly affect the self. Questions such as, 'Should I be agreeing to the after-hours office party tonight?' or thoughts such as, 'I need to get the shirts back from the dry-cleaners now for my husband's presentation tomorrow' or even, 'Should I enrol my daughter in a ballet class or an indoor football one this summer?' Again, each of these questions is valid, important and thus need to be addressed and yet none of them involve you in the element.

It is obvious that almost the entire chunk of our waking hours is spent surfing through the skin of our lives or thinking for others. At the end of the day, we have many doubts and questions that have gone unattended or unanswered.

Introspection or self-observation becomes more critical in our modern life as it has never been before. It links the different activities, thoughts and decisions that we have taken during the day. It brings clarity to our actions and with practice gives direction and a sense of purpose to our life itself. It helps us shed the unnecessary and enables us to travel light in the journey of life.

i) Rationale of the 5-minute questionnaire:

Self-Observation, introspection and self-study or 'Swadhyaya' are often used interchangeably though they have subtle differences. The questionnaire I have provided in the pages that follow will take five minutes out of your life and enable you to see where you are headed from the spiritual perspective. It contains a dozen questions that will act as pointers on where you stand at the moment in terms of a connection with your inner self. More importantly, it will chalk out for you many paths, from which you can choose one or a combination to suit your lifestyle and liking.

The questions are simple and direct requiring an answer either in the affirmative or negative. It is for this reason, only five minutes are allotted to answering the twelve questions.

Five minutes are all that are required from you to get a glimpse of where you could be lacking and what you can do to make your life meaningful and richer in the real sense.

The score range and a brief analysis are provided at end of the questionnaire. The analysis of slabs may vary for those falling on borderlines of score brackets.

But before we answer the 5-minute questionnaire, I expect you to read and understand carefully and above all, answer honestly. It will also provide the basis of further exercises. For this reason, I advise you take the questionnaire with the significance it deserves.

(ii) The 5 minutes towards self-observation – a questionnaire

1. You think about your real purpose in life at least once a month.
   [ ] Yes   [ ] No
2. You are involved in some spiritual activity.
   [ ] Yes   [ ] No
3. You believe in the eternity of the soul.
   [ ] Yes   [ ] No
4. You are spiritual but not religious.
   [ ] Yes   [ ] No
5. You listen to or read or view spiritual content.
   [ ] Yes   [ ] No
6. You are open to spiritual concepts from all parts of the world.
   [ ] Yes   [ ] No
7. You are satisfied with yourself in terms of self-worth, self-esteem and self-image.
   [ ] Yes   [ ] No
8. You meditate at least once a week.
   [ ] Yes   [ ] No
9. You live in harmony with nature.
   [ ] Yes   [ ] No

10. You consistently develop yourself with new tools and skills.
    [ ] Yes   [ ] No
11. You connect to people and nurture relations.
    [ ] Yes   [ ] No
12. You do community work at least once a month.
    [ ] Yes   [ ] No

SCORE

**Number of
'YES' Answers   Meaning**

0 - 4   Your score range hints that you are at the place most people are – busy with their lives and trying to put in calming activities if they fall in your way and you are inclined at the time. Your lifestyle is probably filled with primary responsibility, which is a good thing. However, you need to slow down and do some things for those around you and in turn help yourself get a better and larger perspective on life. This will help you stave off health conditions which may be brewing inside you without your knowledge. You do not need to sweat the small stuff! Read this section of the book.

5 - 8   You are certainly doing very well in terms of movement towards evolution of values. Some of this probably requires making time out for the activities. You are headed in the right direction and will do well to even keep at this level until you feel you are ready to move on to the next level of personal calmness. Such a 'right' time could be the next month or the next decade. However, in moments of dilemmas you tend to lose sight of what resources you could use to your advantage and at other times may momentarily lose faith in your practice. You need to keep at it! See if the book can help you Mentor Your Mind.

9 – 12   You are consciously developing your spiritual values and living most of them. You have the faith and found the calmness you expect from the practices. Being steeped into spirituality you are, at most times, in control of your emotions, mental health and are rooted into equilibrium. Keep it up!

Grounding Yourself in Spiritual Fitness

Let's conduct a simple experiment.

Sit yourself on a chair or a sofa/couch and close your eyes for a minute. Open your eyes and reach for any book or magazine reading it for about two minutes. Observe your feelings.

Now shift yourself to the floor. Sitting down on the ground, close your eyes for a minute and again open your eyes, reaching for the book/magazine and reading it for two minutes. Observe your feelings.

Where were you feeling calmer? Did you feel more content, home-like, and peaceful while seated on the floor? Most would answer with a 'Yes'. Why did that happen?

It is simple. While on the floor, you were connected to the positive energies of the Earth which flowed into your body, which itself is an energy system. Negative energies flowed out. This has been proven using advanced energy measuring devices. This is also called grounding. It a process used almost as a pre-requisite to deeper spiritual processes.

Grounding helps the body connect to the energies of the Earth through the Mooladhar or the first Root Chakra[21] located at the base of the spine denoting the earth element. Grounding helps us create more space within ourselves and open up the world of possibilities for us. Grounding is a

---

21. Muladhara is located at the base of the spine in the vicinity of the coccygeal plexus beneath the sacrum.

technique that continues to grow the more you practice it.

At the symbolic level as well, one needs to ground themselves into a certain minimum of calmness and with gravity to be able to take up spiritual practices.

Grounding essentially gives us the power to heal ourselves, to trust our feelings, to change ourselves and to know our own energy levels and requirements apart from giving us inner calm and strength. Grounding will help us access and get into our body more.

Ancient pundits and gurus have suggested many techniques on how one can ground oneself effectively. Each guru practiced and recommended their own set of exercises. Broadly the knowledge could be categorized into the following practices:

- Be Physically Active
- Eat Natural Foods
- Meditate
- Introspect
- Be Close To Nature Elements
- Practice the Truth
- Find Your Passion and Perfect it
- Avoid Negativity

The pages that follow will provide a brief sketch on what can be done to accomplish spiritual peace and fitness. They cover a range of activities that you can do in your city or town in your busy lives and still achieve the higher goals of life, find the purpose of your life and get closer to the knowledge of the Self.

i. Clean a school or the neighbourhood

When John Wesley said in his sermon in 1778, 'Cleanliness is next to Godliness'; he meant more than just the hygiene element in our surroundings that will help us focus on God more easily. All activities that involve cleaning without the involvement of ego or the expectation of profit/return, done for others or for those that are not explicitly and directly ours cleanses our inner being. It makes us calmer; it keeps in check our false and enlarged egos that cause us inner turmoil. It keeps out envy, pride, dominating and feverish tendencies. In turn, it makes us more peaceful internally, more emotionally stable and puts us in closer touch to our real self. In other words being, staying and keeping your surroundings clean are a symbol of inner and spiritual purity.

If you think you might want to give this line of thought and philosophy some practice to test its validity, you can always volunteer to clean the school you attended or one in your locality or any area of your neighbourhood that you think needs attention on the days the municipal staff have taken an off.

You can speak to the school or neighbourhood authorities to allow you access to its open and visible playground area if not the corridors and classrooms inside and clean it of tissues, disposable glasses, beverage cans, paper and other such litter. If you have a green thumb, you could also ask if you could do some gardening for them.

If your letter of request/intent, back-up documents are genuine and you abide by the authorities' security protocols, they will be glad to have you work for them. It will be a

Grounding Yourself in Spiritual Fitness

win-win situation for both the parties. You could also pool in more people with similar interests by informing them through notices or posting them online.

After getting past the paper and permission formalities, see how you feel after spending an hour doing work that is not yours and without charging for it. In all probability, you will feel exhilarated and contended with life. You would want to talk about it to friends, neighbours, colleagues, acquaintances and involve more people in this idea until it becomes a social movement. It is worth noticing how working for free liberates us and working for a fee keeps us enslaved!

In the following pages we will see how similar activities done purely on a charity or philanthropic platform with altruistic motives makes us more calm, free and enables us see the larger picture in life, our purpose in it, our contribution back to where we take from and helps us rationalize the turmoil that our life brings with ease and comfort.

ii. Community work and karma

What qualifies as community work? In the conventional sense, activity such as that mentioned in the previous pages would be eligible, but with modernization, the scope of community work increases to include:

- Neighbourhood environment
- Neighbourhood watch and protection
- Helping local libraries
- Helping government-run public facility organizations that are short of help

For those living outside of countries where a trash collection has not been developed into recycling categorization, you could start one of your own for your neighbourhood areas. You could collect paper trash on a day, plastic wrapper, disposable glasses, bottles and plate's trash on another day and tin can trash yet another day. You could notify people that you would come around to collect them on certain days and times or if they could keep theirs by their area dustbin in marked packages or leave it by their door in labelled packs.

It would be exciting if you get more people and the young involved in these activities. Besides, making it fun, it will also teach them cleanliness and environment responsibilities. You could talk with or write to your local municipal authority of your initiative and they may provide the required bins and lay out a sanitation system to go with it soon!

Similarly local bodies run by the government such as libraries, post-offices, etc., in the developing nations are generally short of productive staff. You could speak to the authorities and have them allow you to help them in their office work. Remember, all work should be offered free of cost. It will reward you with a new learning of how different workplaces operate their systems of task handling etc. Any experience to be spiritually rewarding and appealing to the higher inner self has to be done selflessly and not in lieu of payment.

iii. Cook and serve food at orphanages

If you reside in a developed country, you can offer free cooking services on Sundays etc., by talking to the orphanage authorities and supplying the necessary paper work to them. You could prepare just a dish for a day.

Orphanages in developing countries support a frugal and minimalistic menu and sometimes also are carbohydrate-based only. You could speak to the authorities and volunteer to bring a dish or cook it there once a week. You could follow a schedule or timetable of your own for the volunteering days and you could also include some vegetable or animal protein in your recipe. This will be a change for the children, fun for the kitchen staff and very satisfying to you.

Another aspect you could delve on is serving. Kitchen staffs often double up to serve the orphans at meal times. Sometimes they are not able to handle the turnout or the disorganised little groups. Your help in getting the children

Grounding Yourself in Spiritual Fitness

to come into the dining hall in order and sit in files and serve them lovingly will be an experience with its own reward. You may have to explain to the children how your doing this will help you help them get food faster and ensure that everyone is served.

There is another route you could take – that of providing groceries (ration supplies or kind) for the orphanage kitchen once a week or funding the kitchen supplies for a day of the week. You can do this if you are short on time or would like to start small on time. You can combine their grocery shopping with your own grocery run so that you do not have to make time for it separately.

iv. Donate knowledge at orphanages etc.

In the ancient Hindu philosophy, the gift of knowledge was ordained as the gift or donation of the highest order. Here 'Knowledge' necessarily meant the attainment of expertise in literature that would bring the devotee or seeker closer to the knowledge of the self or receive enlightenment. It could be arrived at through the learning of any art, science or scripture. Even if looked at from a more modern and materialistic plane, giving knowledge enables the student to lead a better quality of life, more aware of his or her rights and capabilities.

Though a large number of us are employed as teachers and knowledge givers at various schools, colleges and institutions, we are bound by its regimented methods of teaching, following course material within strict timelines and teaching vastly from a non-life approach to subjects.

Think of how it would feel to be able to teach a topic that is of meaning to day-to-day living or whose theme comes in handy to make a living. Here are some invaluable knowledge donation ideas, you can borrow from or come up on your own:

- Teaching skills that will help in day-to-day living:
    - Teaching self grooming and personal hygiene

- Teaching why and how to save
- Teaching how to ride a cycle
- Teaching respect
- Teaching responsibility
- Teaching independence
- Teaching creative skills, examples of which are given under:
- Teaching skills that will help earn a living:
  - Teach a new language
  - Teach how to play a music instrument
  - Teach how to read and write music
  - Teach how to knit, sew, paint, sketch or crafts such as origami etc.
  - Teach cooking, baking

Imagine your sense of fulfilment even if one of your students returns to tell you that you inspired him/her in a way that set them on the path to living a fulfilled life, five years after you are into donating knowledge! Imagine how many lives it is possible to change by setting an example, by teaching a skill, by words and looks of encouragement. To put it very mildly, your cup will brim over.

v. Give away time – old age homes and rehab centres

Unlikely as it seems, time is one of the most valuable gifts one can give away to our children and the seniors of our society. The more we are harried for time, the more it is precious to give. There will never be a time appropriate to think of giving it away, we will have to make time for it. Just as we make time for running groceries, medical check-ups, paying bills, we must give time to the elders around us. Some of them will be lucky to be living with their families but quite a few of them can be found at old-age and senior's homes in the

Grounding Yourself in Spiritual Fitness

city. You only need to make time and visit one to see how much you could do.

As you will find the case with most homes, the old will not be short of cash or facilities. They will be short of love, care, attention – all of which need people's time. It may occur to you that they may have been put in a home because their children had no time to take care of them and their special needs. Though old-age homes do provide the much needed help and relief to the society, they are often devoid of gentleness of love. There are many ways you could help in an old-age home. Some ideas have been short-listed for your benefit:

If you are medically qualified as a nurse or a health care giver such as chiropractic, holistic health therapist, homoeopath etc., you can volunteer to help the residents on days that are off-schedule for them to get a medical consultation. For this you will have to produce the papers, license and other required documents along with an application requesting volunteer services you intend to make available, with the home authorities to seek permission.

- You can volunteer to cook for the residents on the days the kitchen staff is on an off or can assist on some other days. You may also offer help on days they operate with minimal staff in the kitchen.
- If you are good with tools and repairs you could offer maintenance help for the home. Of course, this will require producing the necessary documents to the home authorities for verification.
- Usually old-age homes have some recreational area for activities of residents. You could play with any resident who looks lonely and could do with some distraction or has been requested to by the authorities. A game of carom, ludo, cards, chess always help.
- Think of reading – the residents being older may have trouble reading for long. You could read them

the daily newspaper, the scriptures of choice, classics, jokes- anything that they posses with them or have available in their library.
- You could teach residents to email and the basics computer and the use of internet technology and facility. This will help them keep in touch with their distant and dear ones.
- Women can always share dish recipes, knitting patterns and the like.
- You could help the weak with movements such as getting off the bed or helping them stand, walk, sit, etc.
- You could also help them write letters to their loved ones.
- You could contribute in kind to their reading material, recreation area etc.

vi. Helping the handicapped at special schools

Make time to visit a school or education centre for children with special needs. Apart from the fact that you will be very deeply moved at an emotional level seeing the children trying their best despite their handicaps, you will notice that there is not one type of handicap these centres cater to. Some of the children may have difficulties with motor skills such as handeye coordination, walking, some can use their hands only but are not skilled with leg movements, some have comprehension challenges, some suffer from ADHD/ADD and there will be still others with other challenges to meet and overcome. Think of how you can volunteer to help in these places.

You may want to help their process of integration into the society through any of the skills you possess. If you are trained as a teacher or a special needs assistant, you can prove a valuable asset to such education centres. If you do not possess those skills, you can always volunteer to assist the

Grounding Yourself in Spiritual Fitness

teachers on certain days of week or between certain hours. You can help the challenged pupils with:

- Movement around the class and around in the school
- Understanding concepts
- Meal time feeding and supervision
- Supervision during play hours
- Developing coordinated motor skills for writing
- Recreational activities such as drawing, story-telling, etc.

These are only a few basic ideas. The more you will visit the schools, the closer you will be to such an environment and more ideas will crop up for the ways in which you can contribute to the children's blooming as able individuals.

The contentment and peace, the stability and endurance that will be strongly palpable working in these places is an experience to go through once for every being. In turn it teaches us gratitude for normalcy, grace, humility and enables us to get a panoramic view over parochial thoughts and actions. Most of all it teaches us to make the best out of what we have, to be able to work around our own emotional or mental handicaps. Such lessons in life will not be had from religious scriptures. They are to be experienced through such practices – which make the journey of life, a spiritual one.

vii. Meditation and stillness

The core goal of meditation is to bring about the stillness of mind. Though this is not easy to achieve and takes many years before we reach this destination, meditation practised by people who live everyday lives amidst families, jobs and a society provides a stable and strong base for living a calm life in the middle of all the daily activities, thoughts, decisions and dilemmas. Meditation puts that umbrella over us that protect us from the Sun and rain in our life. It helps us think clearly, alertly, energetically and calmly without getting unduly effected by the external forces that disturb our lives every day.

I have sketched a brief meditation for you that you may practice every day. It is an exercise in self-healing. There are at least two dozen meditations and as many techniques to do them. Here is just one.

i. Sit on a mat on an even floor.
ii. Place your hands on your lap or your palms on the floor – as you find comfortable.
iii. Close your eyes gently.
iv. Inhale slowly and deeply and exhale slowly and completely. Repeat this 6 times.
v. Shift your inner eye to that part of your body that needs healing. It could be a part that is experiencing illness or discomfort at this moment or a part that usually gives you trouble and pain.
vi. Visualise your inner body to be a temple where millions of miniscule volunteers are cleaning the insides and repairing for maintenance.
vii. Now focus on the 'unwell' part of your body, calling thousands of the minute volunteers to clean and repair that part.
viii As they do this, watch them lovingly. Watch the body part lovingly with eyes still closed.
ix. Breathe in deeply and slowly. Divert your fresh and energising breath to the part that needs healing.
x. Stay with Steps vi – ix for at least 7 – 10 minutes.
xi. If your attention wavers elsewhere, bring it back at first awareness.
xii. After your 10 minutes are over, thank the workers sincerely and lovingly for their work and bid them goodbye.

You can alter this meditation to suit your own comfort levels and visualization. The healing improves and picks up pace the more and longer you practice it.

Inner Equanimity: A daily routine

Unlike what most of us visualize, our spiritual journey and growth is not restricted to the elderly and retired of our society and spiritual practices do not mean reading scriptures and attending the prayers at temples most times of the week, though it may comprise a small part of your practice if you so choose. With the passage of time and growth of the human occupational demands, spirituality can and is often adapted to suit the demands of modern day living. It is accessible to all of us and at each moment of the day, whether we live in a monastery or with our family in an urban set-up.

There are a host of little things you can do to begin the passage and travel the beautiful experiential road to spiritual growth. You can infuse your day with the activities I have suggested in the previous pages, you could add little thoughts, actions around your day and home and include a little time for prayer or religious scriptures or just mix and match what you like and what suits your lifestyle. And though, they may not take you all the way to enlightenment immediately, they will set you on the path, so that you may grow from there comfortably, already reasonably grounded in the right thought, behaviour, routines and actions when you do have the time and are in a suitable phase of your life.

Keeping the challenges of everyday living, I have sketched an outline for a schedule you could follow. Of course, you are the better judge to your daily routines and free to move and toss around the activities and times I have mentioned, however, the timetable will give you a brief idea of what extraordinary things can be done by individuals if they are determined to live a life of satiation, inner calm, balance, happiness, emotional and mental strength. I have put 2 schedules in place – one for persons who work or are students and one for homemakers. You will notice that I have put many assumptions in place to make the routine coherent and undemanding. Observe that you could put in as much as an hour and quarter even on a weekday towards your spiritual growth. Take a look and see what you can do!

Working women - activities that you can include in the day

Day	Pre-Breakfast - 15 minutes	On route to Office - Half Hour	Pre-Lunch - 2 minutes	Evening - 10 minutes	Post-Dinner - 15 minutes
Mon	Stretching, Pranayama	Listen to Instrumental music	Short silent prayer of Gratitude	Set your value practice for the week	Introspection, Diary writing
Tue	Stretching, Plant growing work-indoor/outdoor	Listen to Inspirational CDs of social works done by greats of our society	Short silent prayer of Gratitude	Quick list of weekend spiritual activities, make the necessary calls to set appointments	Introspection, Scripture reading
Wed	Stretching, Pranayama	Take 1 spare food packet to give to the needy you find on the way	Short silent prayer of Gratitude	Un-litter the neighbourhood park	Introspection, Diary writing

Inner Equanimity: A daily routine

Day	Pre-Breakfast - 15 minutes	On route to Office - Half Hour	Pre-Lunch - 2 minutes	Evening - 10 minutes	Post-Dinner - 15 minutes
Thu	Stretching, Plant growing work-indoor/outdoor	Write if using public transport, hum if you are driving	Short silent prayer of Gratitude	Check child/senior support online programs	Introspection, Scripture reading
Fri	Stretching, Pranayama	Listen to Instrumental music	Short silent prayer of Gratitude	Remind the authorities of volunteer work you offer and confirm timing	Introspection, Diary writing

Saturdays and Sundays can always be more relaxed and you can dedicate an easier schedule to yourself. You could pick from a variety, though it is advisable not to include them all as you would like a happy balance between family time, a social life, catching up with pending domestic chores, mental and emotional personal times.

You could begin your day with a stretching and guided meditation or Pranayama. You could put on calming, relaxing instrumental music till you prepare your breakfast. Avoid turning on the television or any media that overwhelms us with negative inputs. Take time with your tea or coffee. Go with a calm and giving mind to the place where you want to volunteer – be it an orphanage, an old-age home, a centre for special needs children, the park, library or school. While breaking for lunch, you could read an inspirational book or make quick notes about your experience at the place you just volunteered at. In the evening, you could indulge in growing activities with children or on your own with plants at home or outside. Lastly you could end the day with reading of scriptures of any religion that calm you and look back at the day with a smile and a feeling of satisfaction.

Let's now take a look at what more can be done by those who are home-makers or have young children to look after and these serve as their primary time-consumers of the day. It is amazing how people assume that only those who work at an office keep busy. If you care to peek into the day of a busy home-maker, you may be surprised. She may often be in need of a calming routine but cannot find the time because of the routines of her infant/toddler and chores that revolve around raising a baby. She could find herself challenged for time and soothing nerves. I have put a basic schedule for you as well, mother and home-maker. You do not have to follow the activities charted out – they are only suggestions. You are free to make the changes of days, times and activities to suit your unique life!

Mothers and homemakers – juggling your eggs with ease!

Day	Pre-Breakfast - 10 minutes	After the spouse has left for work	Mid-Morning	Pre-Lunch - 2 minutes	Afternoon	Post-Dinner - 10 minutes
Mon	Stretching	Pranayama	Talk to friends interested in pooling re sources for orphanage charity	Short silent prayer of Gratitude	Sew, bake, knit for sale giving proceeds to charity	Introspection, Diary writing

Inner Equanimity: A daily routine

Day	Pre-Breakfast - 10 minutes	After the spouse has left for work	Mid-Morning	Pre-Lunch - 2 minutes	Afternoon	Post-Dinner - 10 minutes
Tue	Stretching	Plant growing work-indoor/outdoor	Listen to Instrumental music	Short silent prayer of Gratitude	Take 1 spare food packet to give to the needy you find on the way to collect your baby	Introspection, Scripture reading
Wed	Stretching	Pranayama	Visit friends,	Short silent prayer of Gratitude	Collect baby from Day care and Nap	Introspection, Diary writing
Thu	Stretching	Plant growing work-indoor/outdoor	Prayer circle, Satsang	Short silent prayer of Gratitude	Volunteer work, Collect baby from Day care	Introspection, Scripture reading
Fri	Stretching	Pranayama	Listen to Instrumental music	Short silent prayer of Gratitude	Volunteer work, Collect baby from Day care	Introspection, Diary writing

You see how uncomplicated it is to eke out as much as over an hour for practices that will make you more peaceful and will make life more meaningful if not rewarding. Had you been suggested to give an hour to such practices, you would have found the idea impractical if not laughable. It would have been difficult to take such a large slice of time for an activity. But the trick lies in embedding the day with bits and pieces of thoughts and actions that will bring equanimity to your living even though the more serious spiritual practices such as Self-study or 'Swadhaya', deeper contemplation and meditation, silence, complex study of Yoga and scriptures for large chunks of time may not be a possibility for most of us.

It is important to realise and be in 'awareness' that you are blessed despite your challenges for there are always people and living beings in less conducive environments, living lives and in circumstances which are challenges on their own. It is equally important to constantly work at finding a balance of physical, mental, emotional and spiritual growth in our lives. There is no single milestone which when reached spells finality. What is a desired equilibrium today may need to be worked at again after a few months or years to address the changes in our circumstances and the many controllable and uncontrollable elements in our living.

It is a paradox then that to be able to live our lives without regret it is important that we find happiness – much the purpose and meaning of our living, yet happiness is almost never a final destination. To be able to experience happiness it is a pre-requisite to look beyond the imperfections of life, that of others and primarily our own i.e. we must learn to forgive and accept, which itself is an un-'happy' phase. Happiness also almost always demands that you stay in the moment, relishing it to the fullest – even moments of pain, anguish, anger, and sadness – a moment at a time, giving hundred percent in each moment. As author Margaret Lee Runbeck beautifully summarised of living and accepting, "Happiness is not a station to arrive at but a manner of travelling."

Bibliography

Albee, G.W. (1982). Preventing psychopathology and promoting human potential. American Psychologist, 37, 1043-1050.

Alloy, L., Abramson, L., & Chiara, A. (2000). On the mechanisms by which optimism promotes positive mental and physical health. In J. Gillham (ed.) The science of optimism and hope: Research essays in honor of Martin E.P. Seligman (pp. 201-212). Philadelphia: Templeton Foundation Press.

Bandura, A. (1989). Human agency in social cognitive theory. American Psychologist, 14, 175-184.

Barrett, P.M. & Ollendick, T.H. (Eds.). (2004). Handbook of interventions that work with children and adolescents: Prevention and treatment. West Sussex, England: Wiley.

Bromet, E. J. (1998). "Psychiatric Disorders." In *Maxcy-Rosenau-Last Public Health and Preventive Medicine*, 14th edition, ed. Robert B. Wallace. Stamford, CT: Appleton and Lange. Burnt Toast. Author: Teri Hatcher. Publisher: Harper Collins Publishers. ISBN: 9780007229369

Clifford Beers Clinic. (2006, October 30). *About Clifford Beers Clinic*. Retrieved June 1, 2007, from CliffordBeers.org

Clouston, T. C. (1906). *The Hygiene of Mind*.

Cowen, E.L. (1994). The enhancement of psychological wellness: Challenges and opportunities. American Journal of Community Psychology, 22, 149-179.

Csikszentmihalyi, M. (1990) Flow. New York: Harper and Row.

Danner, D., Snowdon, D, & Friesen, W. (2001). Positive emotion in early life and longevity: findings from the nun study. Journal of Personality and Social Psychology, 80, 804-813.

Diagnostic and Statistical Manual of Mental Disorders (DSM IV) (1994), 4th edition. Washington, DC: American Psychiatric Association.

Diener, E. & Diener, C. (1996). Most people are happy. Psychological Science, 3, 181-85.

Eisendrath, S. J., and Lichtmacher, J. (1999). "Psychiatric Disorders." In *Current Medical Diagnosis and Treatment 1999*, eds. L. M. Tierney, Jr., S. J. McPhee, and M. A. Papadakis. Stamford, CT: Appleton and Lange.

Emmons, R. A. & Crumpler, C.A. (2000). Gratitude as a human strength: Appraising the evidence, Journal of Social & Clinical Psychology, 19, 56-69.

Engel, G. (1980). "The Clinical Application of the Biopsychosocial Model." *American Journal of Psychiatry* 137(5):535-544.

Erikson, E. H. (1968). *Identity: Youth and Crisis.*

Evans, D.L., Foa, E.B., Gur, R., Hendrin, H., O'Brien, C., Seligman, M.E.P. & Walsh, B.T. (Eds.). (2005). Treating and preventing adolescent mental health disorders: What we know and what we don't know. New York: Oxford University Press, Annenberg Foundation Trust at Sunnylands, and Annenberg Public Policy Center at the University of Pennsylvania.

Feel the fear and do it anyway. Author: Susan Jeffers. Ph.D. Publishers: Arrow Books. ISBN:0099741008

Fredrickson, B. (2001). The role of positive emotions in positive psychology: The broaden-and-build theory of positive emotions. American Psychologist, 56, 218-226.

Games People Play. Author: Eric Berne M.D. Publisher: Ballantine Books. ISBN: 0345410033

Gardner, H. (1983). Frames of mind: The theory of multiple intelligences. New York: Basic.

Get It Done When You are Depressed. Author(s): Julie A Fast, John D Preston Psy.D, ABPP. Publishers: Alpha (A member of Penguin group USa). ISBN: 9781592577064

Gilbert, D.T., Pinel, E.C., Wilson, T.D., Blumberg, S.J., & Wheatley, T. (1998). Immune neglect: A source of durability bias in affective forecasting. Journal of Personality and Social Psychology, 75, 617-638.

Goodwin, I. (2003). 'The relevance of attachment theory to the philosophy, organization, and practice of adult mental health care'. Clinical Psychology Review, 23/1.

Bibliography

Haidt, J., The Positive emotion of elevation, Prevention & Treatment, 3.

Hales, D., and Hales, R. E. (1995). *Caring for the Mind: The Comprehensive Guide to Mental Health*. New York: Bantam Books.

Hattie, J.A.; Myers, J.E.; Sweeney, T.J. (2004). "A factor structure of wellness: Theory, assessment, analysis and practice". *Journal of Counseling and Development* 82: 354–364.

Heal Your Body. Author: Loiuse L Hay. Publishers: Hay House Inc. ISBN: 9780937611357 and 0937611352

Hibbs, E.D. & Jensen P.S. (Eds.). (1996). Psychosocial treatments for child and adolescent disorders: Empirically based strategies for clinical practice. Washington, D.C.: American Psychological Association.

How To Know God. Author: Deepak Chopra. Publisher: Rider Books. ISBN: 0712605487

Isen, A.M. (1993). Positive affect and decision making. In M. Lewis & J.M. Haviland (Eds.), Handbook of emotions (pp. 261-277). New York: Guilford Press.

Jahoda, M. (1958). Current concepts of positive mental health. New York: Basic Books.

Jamison, K. R. (1999). *Night Falls Fast*. New York: Alfred Knopf.

Johns Hopkins University. (2007). *Origins of Mental Health*. Retrieved June 1, 2007, from JHSPH.edu

Kaplan, Harold I., and Sadock, Benjamin J., eds. (1995). *Comprehensive Textbook of Psychiatry*. 6th edition. Philadelphia: Williams and Wilkins.

Kazdin, A.E. & Weisz, J.R. (2003). Evidence based psychotherapies for children and adolescents. New York: Guilford.

Kendler KS, Neale MC, Kessler RC, et al. Generalized anxiety disorder in women. A population-based twin study. *Archives of General Psychiatry*, 1992; 49(4): 267-72.

Kessler RC, Chiu WT, Demler O, Walters EE. Prevalence, severity, and comorbidity of twelve-month DSM-IV disorders in the National Comorbidity Survey Replication (NCS-R). *Archives of General Psychiatry*, 2005 Jun;62(6):617-27.

Kessler, R. C.; McGonagle, K. A.; Zhao, S.; Nelson, C. B.; Hughes, M.; Eshleman, S.; Wittchen, H. U.; and Kendler, K. S. (1994).

"Lifetime and Twelve Month Prevalence of DSM-III-R Psychiatric Disorders in the United States: Results from the National Comorbidity Study." *Archives of General Psychiatry* 51:8-19.

Keyes, Corey (2002). "The mental health continuum: from languishing to flourishing in life". *Journal of Health and Social Behaviour* 43: 207-222.

King, L.A. & Miner, K.N. (2000). Writing about the perceived benefits of traumatic events: Implications for physical health, Personality and Social Psychology Bulletin, 26, 220-230.

King, L.A. (2001). The health benefits of writing about life goals, Personality and Social Psychology Bulletin, 27, 798-807.

Lyubomirsky, S. (2001). Why are some people happier than others? The role of cognitive and motivational processes in well being. American Psychologist, 56, 239-249.

Lyubomirsky, S., King, L.A. & Diener, E. (2005). The benefits of frequent positive affect: Does happiness lead to success. Psychological Bulletin, 131, 803-855.

Maslow, A.H. (1970). Motivation and personality (2nd ed.). New York: Harper & Row.

Masten, A. (2001). Ordinary magic: resilience processes in development. American Psychologist, 56, 227-238.

Meditation for Beginners. Author: Stephanie Clement. Ph.D. Publishers: Llwellyn Publications. ISBN:9780738702032

Myers, D.G. (2000). The funds, friends, and faith of happy people, American Psychologist, 55, 56-67.

Myers, J.E.; Sweeny, T.J.; Witmer, J.M. (2000). "The wheel of wellness counseling for wellness: A holistic model for treatment planning. Journal of Counseling and Development". *Journal of Counseling and Development* 78: 251-266.

Nathan, P.E. & Gorman, J.M. (1998). A guide to treatments that work. New York: Oxford University Press.

Nathan, P.E. & Gorman, J.M. (2002). A guide to treatments that work (2nd ed.). New York: Oxford University Press.

Office of the Deputy Prime Minister - Social Exclusion Unit: "Factsheet 1: Stigma and Discrimination on Mental Health Grounds".2004.

Parkes, C. M. (2001). *Bereavement* (3rd edn.).

Peterson, C. & Vaidya, R.S. (2003). Optimism as virtue and vice. In E.C. Chang & L.J. Sanna (Eds.), Virtue, vice, and personality: The complexity of behavior (pp. 23-37). Washington, D.C.: American Psychological Association.

Peterson, C. (2006). Primer in positive psychology. New York Oxford University Press.

Princeton University. (Unknown last update). Retrieved June 1, 2007, from Princeton.edu

Richards, P.S.; Bergin, A.E. (2000). *Handbook of Psychotherapy and Religious Diversity*. Washington D.C.: American Psychological Association. p. 4. ISBN 978-1557986245.

Robins LN, Regier DA, eds. *Psychiatric disorders in America: the Epidemiologic Catchment Area Study*. New York: The Free Press, 1991

Rogers, C.R. (1951). Client-centered therapy: Its current practice, implications, and theory. Boston: Houghton Mifflin.

Royal College of Psychiatrists: Changing Minds.

Ryan, R. M. & Deci, E.L. (2000). Self-determination theory and the facilitation of intrinsic motivation, social development, and well-being American Psychologist, 55, 68-78.

Schwartz, B., Ward, A., Monterosso, J., Lyubomirsky, S., White, K., & Lehman, D.R., Maximizing versus satisfying: Happiness is a matter of choice. Journal of Personality and Social Psychology, 83, Nov 2002, 1178-1197.

Seligman, M.E.P. & Pawelski, J.O. (2003). Positive Psychology: FAQs. Psychological Inquiry. 14, 159-163.

Seligman, M.E.P. (1991). Learned Optimism. New York: Knopf.

Seligman, M.E.P. (1994). What you can change and what you can't. New York: Knopf.

Seligman, M.E.P. (2002). Authentic Happiness: Using the New Positive Psychology to Realize Your Potential for Lasting Fulfillment. New York: Free Press/Simon and Schuster.

Seligman, M.E.P., Steen, T.A., Park, N. & Peterson, C. (2005). Positive psychology progress: Empirical validation of interventions. *American Psychologist*, 60, 410-421.

Seligman, Martin E.P.; Csikszentmihalyi, Mihaly (2000). "Positive Psychology: An Introduction". *American Psychologist* 55 (1): 5-14.

Sternberg, R.J. (1985). *Beyond IQ: A triarchic theory of human intelligence.* Cambridge: Cambridge University Press.

Taylor, S.E., Kemeny, M.E., Reed, G.M., Bower, J.E. & Gruenwald, T.L. (2000). Psychological resources, positive illusions, and health. American Psychologist, 55, 99-109.

The Power Is Within You. Author: Louise L Hay. Publishers: Hay House Inc. ISBN:9781561700233

The Power of Self Coaching. Author: Joseph J Luciani Ph.D. Publishers: John Wiley & Sons Inc.

U.S. Public Health Service (1999). *The Surgeon General's Call to Action to Prevent Suicide.* Washington, DC: Author.

Weare, Katherine (2000). *Promoting mental, emotional and social health: A whole school approach.* London: Routledge Falmer. p. 12. ISBN 978-0415168755.

Wilson, D.T., Meyers, J., & Gilbert, D.T. (2001). Lessons from the past: Do people learn from experience that emotional reactions are short-lived. Journal of Personality and Social Psychology, 78, 821-836.

Winner, E. (2000). The origins and ends of giftedness. American Psychologist, 55, 159-169.

Witmer, J.M.; Sweeny, T.J. (1992). "A holistic model for wellness and prevention over the lifespan". *Journal of Counseling and Development* 71: 140-148.

Wootton, B. (1960). *Social Science and Social Pathology.*

World Health Organization (1998). *World Health Report 1998: Life in the Twenty-first Century, A Vision for All.* Report of the Director-General. Geneva: Author.

World Health Organization (2005). Promoting Mental Health: Concepts, Emerging evidence, Practice: A report of the World Health Organization, Department of Mental Health and Substance Abuse in collaboration with the Victorian Health Promotion Foundation and the University of Melbourne. World Health Organization. Geneva.

World Health Report 2001 - Mental Health: New Understanding, New Hope, World Health Organization, 2001